CW00521577

# Active LEARNING
## Curriculum for Excellence

## S1
# MATHEMATICS
## Course Notes

## Edward Mullan

# CONTENTS

# CONTENTS

# SHAPE, POSITION AND MOVEMENT

**PROPERTIES OF 2D SHAPES AND 3D OBJECTS**

**ANGLES, SYMMETRY AND TRANSFORMATION**

# INFORMATION HANDLING

**DATA AND ANALYSIS**

**IDEAS OF CHANCE AND UNCERTAINTY**

# ABOUT THE ACTIVE LEARNING SERIES

Leckie & Leckie's Active Learning series has been developed specifically to help teachers, students and parents implement A Curriculum for Excellence as effectively as possible. Each book is subject-based, written for a specific year group and follows the Outcomes and Experiences, at a level appropriate for that year group. For every subject, both a Course Notes book and an Activity Workbook have been published.

These highly innovative books complement existing class textbooks. They address the Curriculum for Excellence in a thoroughly practical way that makes learning both engaging and fun! A summary of each topic is included before going on to focus on ideas for activities and rich tasks, bringing the topic to life. In line with the principles and philosophies of Curriculum for Excellence, every Course Notes book provides creative ideas for making cross-disciplinary links with other classroom subjects, and, crucially, illustrates the relevance of each topic to everyday life.

The Activity Workbooks present yet more ideas for activities and offer easy to implement suggestions for:

- inter-disciplinary project work,
- topic revision questions,
- an assessment checklist and
- a four capacities mind map.

This ground-breaking new series provides you with a toolkit of ideas, subject links and activities for you to use in the classroom and/or at home.

Leckie & Leckie's Active Learning series – bringing Curriculum for Excellence to life.

# LAYOUT OF YOUR COURSE NOTES BOOK

This Course Notes book covers the third level Outcomes and Experiences. These have been organised into chapters, with a different topic covered on each double page spread.

Every double page spread opens with a knowledge summary for a particular topic which conveys key ideas and concepts. The key topic knowledge is enhanced by a practical example, illustration or case study to reinforce learning. A Top Tip is also included to highlight key information.

Each double page spread also includes the following features:

*Be Active!* column. This column lists questions to assess knowledge and understanding and/or activities to be tried in order to deepen understanding of each topic.

*Make the Link* box. This box highlights the relevance of the topic to a number of other school subjects. This enables learners to gain a more holistic understanding of each topic.

*Our Everyday Lives* box. This box provides an example of how each topic relates to real life, in order to demonstrate its practical relevance.

*Did You Know?* box. This box contains an additional fact about each topic to engage further interest and to bring the subject to life.

# HOW TO USE YOUR COURSE NOTES BOOK

The Course Notes book sets out to provide teachers and students with a valuable toolkit of easy-to-implement ideas for incorporating the philosophies of Curriculum for Excellence into teaching and learning.

The highlighted links with other subjects, activities ideas and real life examples are the perfect starting point for teachers and students to build upon and develop as they explore ideas around a topic. At Leckie & Leckie, our intention is that this Course Notes book will inspire learners to investigate subjects both widely and deeply in practical and creative ways.

Leckie & Leckie welcome further ideas for the Active Learning series and any feedback that you may have. Please write to us at:

Leckie & Leckie
4 Queen Street
Edinburgh EH2 1JE
Email: enquiries@leckieandleckie.co.uk

# ESTIMATION AND ROUNDING

## ROUNDING WHOLE NUMBERS

A newspaper article said, 'The rings of Saturn are 250 000 km in diameter but only 1500 m thick.' The diameter is given to the nearest 10 000 kilometres; the thickness is given to the nearest 100 metres.

Both measurements are given to 2 **significant figures**. In the number 250 000, only the 2 and the 5 are significant. 2 is the most significant; 5 is the least significant.

### RULE

To round off a whole number:
- Set the digits you don't want to zero.
- Check the first digit you set to zero …
  - (i) If it is less than 5 then you have your answer.
  - (ii) Otherwise add 1 to the least significant digit.

6

### EXAMPLE 1

Round 23 471 to the nearest thousand.

**Response**
23 000
The first digit discarded is a 4 … which is less than 5
Final answer: 23 000

23 471 lies between 23 000 and 24 000 and is closer to 23 000

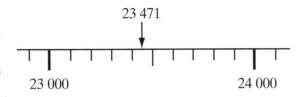

**TOP TIP**
If a number is exact then all the digits are significant.
The 50 on a 50p piece is exact … two significant figures.

### EXAMPLE 2

Round 23 624 to the nearest thousand.

**Response**
24 000
The first digit discarded is a 6 … which is **not** less than 5
Final answer: 24 000

23 624 lies between 23 000 and 24 000 and is closer to 24 000

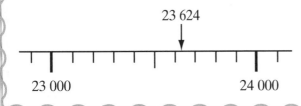

**E ACTIVE**

## QUICK TEST

1. Round the following whole numbers to the nearest 10
   (a) 346  (b) 592  (c) 795  (d) 3456

2. Round the following numbers to 2 decimal places
   (a) 5·673  (b) 0·219  (c) 0·015  (d) 9·0067

3. Round the following numbers to 2 significant figures
   (a) 7342  (b) 4·85  (c) 0·0277  (d) 0·001386

## QUICK TASKS

- If you have access to a computer with a spreadsheet, explore the INT function.

  What will happen when you type =INT(3.6251) into a cell?

  What about =INT(3.6251 + 0.5)?
  ... or =INT(3.6251 * 10 + 0.5)/10? (note * means multiply; / means divide)

  How would you get the spreadsheet to round to two decimal places?

# NUMBER, MEASURE AND MONEY

## MAKE THE LINK

- **Craft and Design** – tolerance.
- **Physics** – measuring error; confidence in result.
- **IT** – programming a computer to round.

## DID YOU KNOW?

In a decimal, leading zeros are **not** significant.

All the digits after the first significant digit are also significant ... In 0·001020 there are 4 significant figures ... 1020.

## OUR EVERYDAY LIVES:

In real life whether to round up or down often **does not depend on the rules** but on the practical nature of the story:

### Example

Seven friends wish go to the airport by taxi. A taxi can carry five passengers. How many taxis are needed?

7 ÷ 5 = 1·4. To the nearest whole number this rounds to 1 (according to the rule.)  But ordering 1 taxi would lead to 2 friends being left behind. So we need to round **up** to 2 taxis for practical reasons.

# ESTIMATION AND ROUNDING

## ROUNDING TO A FIXED NUMBER OF DECIMAL PLACES

### RULE

- Score out the digits you don't want.

- Note the first digit you lose.
  (i)  If it is less than 5 ... round down.
  (ii)  Otherwise round up.

### EXAMPLE 1

Divide 10 by 7 on your calculator and you'll get 1.428571429 ...

If we only want 1 decimal place, score out what we don't want ... 1.4~~28571429~~ ... the answer lies between 1·4 and 1·5

... the first digit being lost is '2'

... this is less than 5

... choose the lower option.

To 1 decimal place 1·428571429 = 1·4

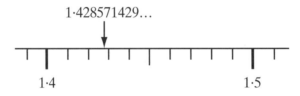

### EXAMPLE 2

If we want 3 decimal places ... 1.428~~571429~~

the answer lies between 1·428 and 1·429

... the first digit being lost is '5'

... this is not less than 5

... choose the higher option.

To 3 decimal places 1·428571429 = 1·429

## BE ACTIVE

### QUICK TASKS

- When you round off, you create an estimate of the correct answer ... and introduce what's called **a rounding error**. 3·1415926 = 3·14 ( to 2 d.p.) with a rounding error 0·0015926.

  If you are asked to do the following calculation 16 ÷ 7 × 100, why would it be silly to round off the result of 16 ÷ 7 to 2 decimal places before multiplying by 100?

- How could you use rounding to estimate the answer to 37 × 18 ÷ 21?

- A joiner measures a length of rod as 24·7 cm.

  All he really knows is that the rod is between 24·65 cm and 24·75 cm long.

  He measures along the rod 17·3 cm and saws off a piece of wood.

  Again, all he really knows is that he's made the cut between 17·25 cm and 17·35 cm along the rod.

  You would think that the bit that's cut off is 24·6 – 17·3 = 7·3 cm long.

  In what range does the actual length lie?

  Explore errors in measurement.

# NUMBER, MEASURE AND MONEY

## MAKE THE LINK

- **Economics** – foreign exchange and rounding to 2 d.p.

- **Geography** – 4-figure grid references versus 6-figure grid references

- **PE** – timing races; accuracy and precision

- **Mathematics** – analysing errors

## DID YOU KNOW?

In any serious science experiment which involves calculations, a note of the effect of rounding errors on the findings is made.

**9**

## OUR EVERYDAY LIVES:

In real life whether to round up or down often does not depend on the rules but on the practical nature of the story:

**Example**
iTunes let you download songs at 79p per track. Michael has £10. How many tracks can he download?

10 ÷ 0·79 = 12·6582278 which rounds to 13 (according to the rules)
Now, 13 × 0·79 = 10·27 ... but Michael doesn't have £10·27.
So we need to round down to 12 tracks for practical reasons.

# ADDITION, SUBTRACTION, MULTIPLICATION AND DIVISION

## VOCABULARY

**The sum:** You tend to add when you see the keywords 'sum', 'total', 'together'.

**The difference:** You tend to subtract when you see the keywords 'difference', 'minus'.

**The product:** Is the result of a multiplication. Because it is repeated addition, the keywords for addition can also appear.

**The quotient:** Is the result of a division. Sharing out or reversing multiplication are the most common places to find quotients in problems.

## EXAMPLE 1

Marion, Jeff and Drew each had different things for lunch. Their bills were £3·45, £4·27, and £2·90. They agreed just to share the total bill equally. How much did they each pay?

**Response**

We need a total: 3·45 + 4·27 + 2·90 = 10·62
... to share among 3:  10·62 ÷ 3 = 3·54
Each person paid £3·54.

## EXAMPLE 2

Last week you could get 1·45 euros (€) to the pound (£).
This week you would get 0·12 euros less.
How many euros will you get this week for £45?

**Response**

Work out the difference: 1·45 – 0·12 = 1·33
... then find the product: 1·33 × 45 = 59·85
You will get €59·85.

## EXAMPLE 3

Marg wanted to buy 30 DVDs but was told that this would cost £277·50.
She only had £240·50.
How many DVDs could she buy for that?

**Response**

Divide to find the cost of one DVD:
277·50 ÷ 30 = 9·25
Divide to find how many 9·25s are in 240·50:
240·50 ÷ 9·25 = 26
She could afford 26 DVDs.

**TOP TIP**

Always show clearly whether you are adding, subtracting, multiplying or dividing ... and always give your answer to the right degree of accuracy.

**TOP TIP**

The more you practise without a calculator, the better you'll get.

10

**BE ACTIVE**

## QUICK TESTS

1. When three cars were parked nose-to-tail on a car ferry they occupied a space 12·26 m long. Two of the cars had lengths 3·91 m and 4·20 m. What was the length of the third?

2. Seventeen daily journeys on the bus cost a commuter £106·25. What would 24 such journeys cost him?

3. Frank and Ella went shopping with a £100 note. Frank bought an MP3 player at £34·89 and Ella bought an electronic diary costing £41·27. They agreed to share the change evenly. How much did each get?

## QUICK TASKS

- Try to estimate what materials your class will need to do maths for the coming year. Play the part of the principal teacher and work out the total cost of the pencils, rulers, jotters, etc that you will need.

  Look in the catalogues for bargains when you buy in bulk.

- Look at the first example in the quick test. Can you type a formula into a spreadsheet cell which will produce the answer? How about questions 2 and 3? Explore how formulae are entered and built up in spreadsheets using (,), +, −, *, /

- Numbers have many curious properties. Use a calculator to help you explore division by 7.
  $1 \div 7 =$
  $2 \div 7 =$
  $3 \div 7 =$
  etc.
  Pay attention to the pattern of digits.
  What has it to do with the hexagon shown?

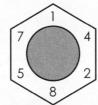

# NUMBER, MEASURE AND MONEY

## MAKE THE LINK

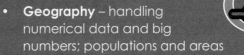

- **Geography** – handling numerical data and big numbers; populations and areas
- **History** – Roman numerals and the difficulty of manipulation
- **Science** – scientists need a good grasp of the four rules
- **IT** – explore the four rules in spreadsheets
- **Mathematics** – many of the foundations of mathematics are laid here
- **English** – the skill of close reading!

## DID YOU KNOW?

It is estimated that credit card fraud costs £330 for every person in Scotland per year. The population of Scotland is 5 100 000. This number is given to two significant figures. To work out the estimated total cost of credit card fraud in Scotland you would do the following sum: £330 × 5 100 000 = £1 683 000 000 which is £1 700 000 000 to 2 s.f.

## OUR EVERYDAY LIVES:

When you add, subtract, multiply or divide … you can't end up with an answer that is more accurate than the original data.

### Example
The Glastonbury Festival has been running since 1970, when 1400 fans attended. In 2008, 177 400 turned out.
a) How accurate do you think these figures are?
b) What has been the increase in attendance between 1970 and 2008?

*Response*
a) The numbers are given to the nearest 100.
b) 177 400 − 1400 = 176 000 to the nearest hundred
   i.e. 1760 hundred

# NUMBER FACTS

## THE BASICS

1. When adding or subtracting, position the numbers so that the decimal points line up.

   **Example** 23·75 + 314·2

**Response**

$$\begin{array}{r} 23{\cdot}75 \\ 314{\cdot}2 \\ \hline 337{\cdot}95 \end{array}$$

2. You should memorise the multiplication tables … it is useful to know up to 12 × 12.

## EXAMPLE

| | 1 | 2 | 3 | 4 | 5 | 6 | 7 | 8 | 9 | 10 | 11 | 12 |
|---|---|---|---|---|---|---|---|---|---|---|---|---|
| 1 | 1 | 2 | 3 | 4 | 5 | 6 | 7 | 8 | 9 | 10 | 11 | 12 |
| 2 | 2 | 4 | 6 | 8 | 10 | 12 | 14 | 16 | 18 | 20 | 22 | 24 |
| 3 | 3 | 6 | 9 | 12 | 15 | 18 | 21 | 24 | 27 | 30 | 33 | 36 |
| 4 | 4 | 8 | 12 | 16 | 20 | 24 | 28 | 32 | 36 | 40 | 44 | 48 |
| 5 | 5 | 10 | 15 | 20 | 25 | 30 | 35 | 40 | 45 | 50 | 55 | 60 |
| 6 | 6 | 12 | 18 | 24 | 30 | 36 | 42 | 48 | 54 | 60 | 66 | 72 |
| 7 | 7 | 14 | 21 | 28 | 35 | 42 | 49 | 56 | 63 | 70 | 77 | 84 |
| 8 | 8 | 16 | 24 | 32 | 40 | 48 | 56 | 64 | 72 | 80 | 88 | 96 |
| 9 | 9 | 18 | 27 | 36 | 45 | 54 | 63 | 72 | 81 | 90 | 99 | 108 |
| 10 | 10 | 20 | 30 | 40 | 50 | 60 | 70 | 80 | 90 | 100 | 110 | 120 |
| 11 | 11 | 22 | 33 | 44 | 55 | 66 | 77 | 88 | 99 | 110 | 121 | 132 |
| 12 | 12 | 24 | 36 | 48 | 60 | 72 | 84 | 96 | 108 | 120 | 132 | 144 |

The main diagonal gives you the square numbers.

You should be able to see that the symmetry in the table comes from the fact that a × b = b × a. For example 2 × 4 has the same value as 4 × 2.

**TOP TIP**

Multiplication and division are opposite sides of the same coin … make sure the multiplication tables are well practised.

3. Prepare the ground for long division by making a multiplication table of the divisor.

## EXAMPLE

**Example**

What is 4897·02 ÷ 17?

Step 1: Set up a 17 times table

| 1 | 2 | 3 | 4 | 5 | 6 | 7 | 8 | 9 |
|---|---|---|---|---|---|---|---|---|
| 17 | 34 | 51 | 68 | 85 | 102 | 119 | 136 | 153 |

Step 2: Set up the division

17 ⟌ 48 97·02

48 ÷ 17 … the table tells us 2 times

$$\begin{array}{r} 2 \\ 17\,\overline{)\,4897{\cdot}02} \\ 34 \\ \hline 1497{\cdot}02 \end{array}$$

149 ÷ 17 … the table tells us 8 times

$$\begin{array}{r} 28 \\ 17\,\overline{)\,4897{\cdot}02} \\ 34 \\ \hline 1497{\cdot}02 \\ 136 \\ \hline 137{\cdot}02 \end{array}$$

137 ÷ 17 … the table tells us 8 times
10 ÷ 17 … the table tells us 0 times
102 ÷ 17 … the table tells us 6 times

$$\begin{array}{r} 288{\cdot}06 \\ 17\,\overline{)\,4897{\cdot}02} \\ 34 \\ \hline 1497{\cdot}02 \\ 136 \\ \hline 137{\cdot}02 \\ 136 \\ \hline 1{\cdot}02 \end{array}$$

4897·02 ÷ 17 = 288·06

## BE ACTIVE

### QUICK TESTS

1. Add 3·45, 17·6 and 28 without a calculator.

2. Calculate 37·45 – 9·6.

3. 4 × 4 × 4 = 64. 64 is called the cube of 4.

   Calculate the cubes of all the numbers from 1 × 1 × 1 to 10 × 10 × 10.

4. Divide 163·02 by 13.

### QUICK TASKS

- The 'times' tables are full of patterns. Exploring these can only strengthen your grip.

  (i) Most folk find the 2-times table and the 5-times table easy ... but get stuck on the 7-times table. What's the connection between these three tables?

  (ii) Go down the 9-times table adding together the digits of each answer. What do you notice?

     What's the connection between the 10s digit in the answer and the digit being multiplied by 9?

- Google 'multiply using your fingers' to find a good trick to help you remember your tables.

- Explore how to generate the 'times' tables on a spreadsheet.

  Can you get the spreadsheet to make the table at the start of this section by entering one formula only and then filling to the right and then filling down?

# NUMBER, MEASURE AND MONEY

## MAKE THE LINK

- **Science** – these particular skills are 'ubiquitous', which means they 'are to be found everywhere'. Don't depend on your calculator when doing calculations in other subjects ... the more you practise without it the better you get. This is just as true in mathematics as it is in sports.

## DID YOU KNOW?

We can only manipulate figures easily on paper because in the past we stopped using Roman numerals (such as I, II, III and IV) and moved over to the Indo-Arabic system where we use 10 digits (0, 1, 2, 3, 4 etc) and the position of the digits is important. Investigate the mathematician 'Leonardo of Pisa' and find out his role in this change.

## OUR EVERYDAY LIVES:

Many shops use ready-reckoners to help you calculate costs. A ready-reckoner is a table which usually shows the cost of 1 to 9 items and the cost of 10, 20, 30, ..., 90 items. The shopper can then work out the cost of any number from 1 to 99 by simple addition ... avoiding multiplication.

# NEGATIVE NUMBERS

## WORKING WITH NUMBERS THAT ARE LESS THAN ZERO

When you work with negative numbers, imagine or even draw a vertical number-line. That way 'below zero' has a bit of extra meaning.

### ADDITION

To add two numbers on the number-line ... start at the first number and treat the second number as an instruction to move.

**Examples:**
4 + 3 ... start at 4 and go up 3 ... end up at 7
4 + (–3) ... start at 4 and go down 3 ... end up at 1

### THE NEGATIVE OF A NUMBER

**Examples:**
The negative of 4 is –4; the negative of –4 is 4.

### SUBTRACTION

Subtracting a number is the same as adding the negative of the number.

**Examples:**
4 – 3 = 4 + (–3) ... start at 4 and go down 3 ... end up at 1
4 – (–3) = 4 + 3 ... start at 4 and go up 3 ... end up at 7
–4 – 3 = –4 + (–3) ... start at –4 and go down 3 ... end up at –7
–4 – (–3) = –4 + 3 ... start at –4 and go up 3 ... end up at –1

### MULTIPLICATION

- Look at this pattern
  $3 \times 1 = 3; 2 \times 1 = 2; 1 \times 1 = 1; 0 \times 1 = 0$
  ... and continuing the pattern we get $-1 \times 1 = -1$

- Using similar patterns we see that we can get the negative of a number by multiplying by –1 ... e.g. $-4 = -1 \times 4; 4 = -1 \times (-4)$

- Two positives: $3 \times 4 = 12$
  A positive and a negative: $-3 \times 4 = -1 \times 3 \times 4 = -1 \times 12 = -12$
  Two negatives: $-3 \times (-4) = -1 \times 3 \times (-1) \times 4 = 1 \times 12 = 12$

The number-line on the right reads, top to bottom: 7, 6, 5, 4, 3, 2, 1, 0, –1, –2, –3, –4, –5, –6, –7, –8, –9.

## EXAMPLES

*Rules*

- **A rule for multiplying <u>two</u> integers:**

  When the signs are the same the product is positive
  When the signs are different the product is negative.

  (a) $2 \times 3 = 6$   (b) $2 \times (-3) = -6$   (c) $-2 \times 3 = -6$   (d) $-2 \times (-3) = 6$

- **A similar rule works for division.**

  When the signs are the same the quotient is positive
  When the signs are different the quotient is negative.

  (a) $6 \div 3 = 2$   (b) $6 \div (-3) = -2$   (c) $-6 \div 3 = -2$   (d) $-6 \div (-3) = 2$

**TOP TIP**

The result of a multiplication is called a **product**; the result of a division is called a **quotient**.

14

## BE ACTIVE

## QUICK TESTS

1. Calculate:
   (a) 3 + (–6)  (b) –2 + (–3)  (c) –4 + 1
   (d) –2 + (–1) + 5

2. Evaluate:
   (a) 5 – (–2)  (b) –6 – 3  (c) –3 – (–1)
   (d) 1 – (–1) + 2

3. Evaluate the products:
   (a) –5 × 2  (b) –3 × (–6)  (c) 7 × (–2)
   (d) –9 × (–9)

4. Calculate:
   (a) –15 ÷ 3  (b) –3 ÷ (–1)  (c) 28 ÷ (–7)
   (d) –7 ÷ (–2)

## QUICK TASKS

- What's the difference in height between the Sea of Galilee and Schiphol Airport (Amsterdam)?

  See if you can find other places which are below sea level.

  Can you find one in Britain?

- Rotation, in mathematics, makes use of negative numbers. To turn through –90° is to turn through 90° clockwise; to turn through 45° is to turn through 45° anti-clockwise. Note that turning through –90° produces the same effect as rotating 270°.

- On a computer open a Word document.

  Use the drawing tools to give you an arrow:

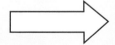

  Double click the arrow ... you can alter the fill colour and the line colour:

  Choose 'size' from the menu that pops up when you double-clock and experiment with 'rotation' by putting different positive and negative angles into the box.

  Double-click on the arrow that you set to –90° ... what does the rotation box read?

  Write a report comparing the computer's use of negative numbers in rotation with that of maths.

# NUMBER, MEASURE AND MONEY

## MAKE THE LINK

- **Geography** – the use of sea level as zero elevation leads to a natural place for negative numbers to occur; latitude and longitude: using the convention that west is negative we need only divide the longitude by –15 to find the time difference.

- **English** – The word 'minus' has been considered a verb until fairly recently with 'negative' being the adjective. Heather the Weather will refer to a temperature of 'minus 4' when 'negative 4' is meant.

## DID YOU KNOW?

All heights are measured from sea level. This is defined as halfway between high tide and low tide in the open ocean. The shores of the Dead Sea form one of the few pieces of land that is actually below sea level ... its height is negative. As you walk towards the Dead Sea from sea level, your height drops by 3 metres for every kilometre you travel. After 20 km your height is 20 × (–3) = –60 ... you are 60 m below sea level.

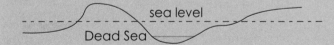

sea level

Dead Sea

15

## OUR EVERYDAY LIVES:

The *goal difference* is quite important to a football team. Goals 'for' are considered positive and goals 'against' negative. We find the goal difference by adding the for and against scores. e.g 8 goals for and 3 goals against... 8 + (–3) = 5. The goal difference is 5.

Thermometers also make use of positive and negative numbers. For example, one day a thermometer reads –2°C. The next day it reads 3°C. 3 – (–2) = 5 ... the temperature has gone up by 5°.

# MULTIPLES AND FACTORS

## TESTS FOR DIVISIBILITY

The following quick tests are useful:

- A number can be divided by 2 if its last digit is even.
- A number is divisible by 3 if its **digital root** can be divided by 3. (To find the digital root, sum the digits. If the result has more than 1 digit, sum these digits. Repeat until you only have one digit, e.g. 3451987 has a digital root of 3 + 4 + 5 + 1 + 9 + 8 + 7 = 37 ; 3 + 7 = 10; 1 + 0 = 1 ... the digital root is 1.)
- A number can be divided by 4 if its last two digits can be divided by 4.
- A number can be divided by 5 if its last digit is 0 or 5.
- There is no easy test for 7 that isn't just division by 7 in disguise.
- A number can be divided by 6 if it can be divided by 2 and 3.
- A number can be divided by 8 if its last three digits can be divided by 8.
- A number can be divided by 9 if its digital root is 9.
- A number can be divided by 10 if its last digit is zero.

## COMMON FACTORS

When one number divides a second without remainder, the first is called a **factor** or **divisor** of the second.

### EXAMPLE

$36 \div 4 = 9$ so 4 is a factor of 36.

$48 \div 4 = 12$ so 4 is a factor of 48.

Note 1, 2, 3, 4, 6, 9, 12, 18, 36 are all factors of 36.

1, 2, 3, 4, 6, 8, 12, 16, 24, 48 are all factors of 48.

1, 2, 3, 4, 6, 12 are common to both lists.

12 is the greatest of these.

12 is the greatest common divisor of 36 and 48.

We say the GCD of 36 and 24 is 12, or the *greatest common divisor* of 36 and 48.

Listing the divisors to find the GCD is fine when the numbers are not too big ... but what is the GCD of 1358 and 6874?

**TOP TIP**

When you divide the bigger number by the smaller then the GCD of the two numbers is the same as the GCD of the smaller number and the remainder in the division.

The Top Tip can make GCD problems easier.

**Example**

Find the GCD of 1358 and 6874.

$6874 \div 1358 = 5$ remainder 84 ... we now want the GCD of 1358 and 84.

$1358 \div 84 = 16$ remainder 14 ... we now want the GCD of 84 and 14.

$84 \div 14 = 6$ remainder 0 ... we now want the GCD of 14 and 0 ... the GCD is 14.

## COMMON MULTIPLES

For the purposes of this section when we multiply the list 1, 2, 3, 4 ... by a number we obtain the multiples of that number.

The multiples of 3 are 3, 6, 9, 12, 15, 18, 21, 24, 27, 30, 33, ...

## E ACTIVE

### UICK TESTS

1. Find the greatest common factor (GCD) of
   (a) 14 and 49  (b) 125 and 79  (c) 208 and 1712  (d) 378 and 8442
2. Find the lowest common multiple (LCM) of
   (a) 3 and 25  (b) 21 and 35  (c) 18 and 42 (d) 36 and 99
3. Mrs Simpson is having a party for her children. She has a bottle with 1066 ml of orange juice and another with 2054 ml of apple juice. What is the biggest portion she can create so that all portions are the same size and there is no waste nor need for mixing? (Hint: we want the GCD of 1066 and 2054.)
4. In one school the bell rang every 40 minutes. In another it rang every 48 minutes. If they both ring at 9 a.m. will they ring together at any other time that day?

### UICK TASKS

- Working with spreadsheets, it's good to know that =GCD(36, 24) will give you 12 and =LCM(36, 24) will give you 72. If they don't work you may have to go to Tools > Add-ins… select Analysis Toolpack and click OK. Then they'll work.
- How might you figure out the LCM of 3 numbers? Write a set of instructions.
- You have two lengths which are 133 cm and 511 cm long. You want to invent a new ruler with a unit bigger than the centimetre. This ruler should measure both lengths in a whole number of your new unit of measurement. Can you invent such a ruler?
- Galileo discovered that four moons orbited Jupiter. Measuring in tenths of a day, the time it takes each moon to orbit Jupiter is given in the table:

| Moon | Time |
| --- | --- |
| Io | 18 |
| Europa | 36 |
| Ganymede | 72 |
| Callisto | 162 |

On a certain date, the 4 moons lined up. Explore when this will happen again. Write a report on how you found your answer.

## MAKE THE LINK

- **Mathematics** – the LCM is used wherever we need to add, subtract or compare the sizes of or simplify fractions.

- **Chemistry** – Dalton's atomic theory states that atoms combine in simple whole-number ratios to form molecules. These ratios can be simplified by using the LCM.

- **Science** – as can be seen from the Jupiter example in the Quick Tasks, the LCM can be used to look at problems where the movement of things is regular.

- **Home Economics** – as in the example with the orange and apple juice, the GCD can be used to efficiently divide different items into a common measure.

17

## DID YOU KNOW?

The LCM of two numbers, say 125 and 15, can be worked out by dividing their product by their GCD This tip gives another method useful for big numbers.
First find the GCD … 125 ÷ 15 = 8 remainder 5; 15 ÷ 5 = 3 remainder 0; 5 is GCD.
LCM = 125 × 15 ÷ 5 = 375

## OUR EVERYDAY LIVES:

Suppose you had a wall which measured 1358 cm by 6874 cm.
What is the biggest size of square tile that will cover the wall without needing to cut tiles?
The biggest number which divides both these lengths is their GCD … 14.
14 × 97 = 1358; 14 × 491 = 6874
You need tiles of side 14 cm.
(You'll need 97 tiles by 491 tiles.)

# PRIME NUMBERS AND POWERS

## COUNTING THE FACTORS

| | |
|---|---|
| 1 has only 1 factor … 1 | 2 has two factors … 1 and 2 |
| 3 has 2 factors … 1 and 3 | 4 has 3 factors … 1, 2 and 4 |
| 5 has 2 factors … 1 and 6 | 6 has 4 factors … 1, 2, 3 and 6 |
| 7 has 2 factors … 1 and 7 | 8 has 4 factors … 1, 2, 4 and 8 |
| 9 has 3 factors … 1, 3 and 9 | 10 has 4 factors … 1, 2, 5 and 10 |
| 11 has 2 factors … 1 and 11 | 12 has 6 factors … 1, 2, 3, 4, 6 and 12 |

- 1 is the only whole number with 1 factor.
- Square numbers are the only numbers with an odd number of factors.
- We call the numbers which have exactly two factors **prime numbers**.
- Numbers with more than two factors are called **composite numbers**.

## EXAMPLE

A good method of finding primes is called the **Sieve of Eratosthenes**.

Here's how to sieve out the primes from the numbers up to 100.

Step 1    List the numbers from 1 to 100. Score out 1. It's not prime.

Step 2    2 is the next number. Circle it and score out all the numbers that can be divided by 2.

Step 3    3 is not scored out. Circle it and score out the numbers which can be divided by 3.

Step 4    Circle the next number which is not scored out. Score out its multiples.

Step 5    Repeat step 4 until you go by 10. (10 × 10 = 100 … we don't need to search further.)

Step 6    All the numbers circled or not scored out are the prime numbers up to 100.

Here is the table after all the steps are complete.

| 1 | ② | ③ | 4 | ⑤ | 6 | ⑦ | 8 | 9 | 10 |
|---|---|---|---|---|---|---|---|---|---|
| ⑪ | 12 | ⑬ | 14 | 15 | 16 | ⑰ | 18 | ⑲ | 20 |
| 21 | 22 | ㉓ | 24 | 25 | 26 | 27 | 28 | ㉙ | 30 |
| ㉛ | 32 | 33 | 34 | 35 | 36 | ㊲ | 38 | 39 | 40 |
| ㊶ | 42 | ㊸ | 44 | 45 | 46 | ㊼ | 48 | 49 | 50 |
| 51 | 52 | ㊼53 | 54 | 55 | 56 | 57 | 58 | ㊾59 | 60 |
| ㊱61 | 62 | 63 | 64 | 65 | 66 | ㊸67 | 68 | 69 | 70 |
| ㊼71 | 72 | ㊴73 | 74 | 75 | 76 | 77 | 78 | ㊾79 | 80 |
| 81 | 82 | ㊱83 | 84 | 85 | 86 | 87 | 88 | ㊾89 | 90 |
| ㊱91 | 92 | 93 | 94 | 95 | 96 | ㊲97 | 98 | 99 | 100 |

**TOP TIP**

To check if a number is prime you must try to divide it by all the primes less than or equal to the **square root** of the number.

## PRIME FACTORISATION

When you break a number down into a multiplication you do so by factorising.

When you continue to break it down till it ends up all primes … this is called prime factorisation

e.g. 600 = 2 × 300 = 2 × 2 × 150  = 2 × 2 × 2 × 75 = 2 × 2 × 2 × 3 × 25

= 2 × 2 × 2 × 3 × 5 × 5

Thus 600 = 2 × 2 × 2 × 3 × 5 × 5 [This is often written $2^3 × 3 × 5^2$.]

Apart from the order of the terms, this is the only way to break 600 up into primes.

This is true for any number … there's only one way of getting its prime factorisation.

The prime factors of 600 are 2, 3 and 5.

## BE ACTIVE

### QUICK TESTS

1. Test each of these to decide if they are prime numbers.
   (a) 151  (b) 349  (c) 1181  (d) 1191
2. Evaluate:
   (a) $4^3$  (b) $2^6$  (c) $5^2$  (d) $6^3$
3. Use prime factorisation to find the GCD of 16170 and 4140

### QUICK TASKS

- It is known that all prime numbers are one more or one less than a multiple of 6. e.g. 37 is prime; 61 is prime … Explore whether the reverse is also true … i.e. if I add 1 to any multiple of 6 will I get a prime number?

- If you think you're good enough, make your own prime searcher using Excel.
  Open a blank Excel sheet.
  In the menu bar follow the trail
  **Tools > Macro > Visual Basic Editor**
  then **Insert > Module**
  and type the following into the small blank page that appears.
  'End Function' will type itself.
  Press <RETURN> to get to the next line

```
Function prime(n)
If Int(n / 2) = n / 2 Then n = n - 1
flag = 1
Do While flag = 1
n = n + 2
flag = 0
For x = 3 To Int(Sqr(n)) Step 2
If Int(n / x) = n / x Then flag = 1
Next x
If flag = 0 Then prime = n
Loop
End Function
```

Once it's all typed …
Go to the menu bar and follow
**Excel > Close and return to Microsoft Excel.**
Save your sheet.
Now when you click on a cell and type '= prime(**n**)' where **n** is a whole number bigger than 1, the prime number just bigger than **n** will appear.
Even better … in cell A1 enter '2'; in cell A2 enter ' =prime(A1)' … 3 will appear … it's the next prime after 2
Now select A2 and fill down … the list of primes will appear.

## MAKE THE LINK

- **Mathematics** – primes are so specialised that their main use is in mathematics itself. For example, we know from above that the prime factors of $600 = 2^3 \times 3^1 \times 5^2$. Add 1 to each power to get 4, 2, 3 and multiply these to get 24… 600 will have 24 factors. Can you find them all?

- **IT** – primes are used in security procedures on the web; without this security most on-line finance would not take place.

## DID YOU KNOW?

We can use prime factorisation as another way to find the GCD of numbers.

**Example**
Find the GCD of 1176 and 8330
$1176 = 2 \times 2 \times 2 \times 3 \times 7 \times 7$
$8330 = 2 \times 5 \times 7 \times 7 \times 17$
The two prime factorisations share $2 \times 7 \times 7$, so the GCD is 98.

19

## OUR EVERYDAY LIVES:

Powers are a useful shorthand for repeated multiplication.
$3 \times 3 = 3^2$ (read as '3 squared');
$6 \times 6 \times 6 = 6^3$ (read as '6 cubed');
$5 \times 5 \times 5 \times 5 = 5^4$ (read as '5 to the power 4')

To work these powers out on a calculator a special button is provided.
It can take various forms … check out *your* calculator …
**3 x$^y$ 4** = … will work out $3 \times 3 \times 3 \times 3 = 81$
Your calculator may show **3 y$^x$ 4** =
or even **3 ∧ 4** =
This last one is the one used by Excel.

# FRACTIONS, DECIMALS AND PERCENTAGES

## REMINDERS

- A common fraction such as $\frac{3}{4}$ can be looked on as a number ... the answer to the division $3 \div 4$, i.e. $0{\cdot}75$

  For that reason we say that $\frac{3}{4}$ is equivalent to $0{\cdot}75$.

- In the same way a number can be written as a fraction ... $16 = 16 \div 1 = \frac{16}{1}$

- Other divisions also produce the answer $0{\cdot}75$ e.g. $\frac{6}{8}, \frac{9}{12}, \frac{12}{16}, \frac{15}{20}, \frac{18}{24}, \ldots$

  These are all equivalent to $\frac{3}{4}$.

  Note that, for example in the case of $\frac{18}{24}$, the GCD of 18 and 24 is 6 ... $\frac{18}{24} = \frac{6 \times 3}{6 \times 4} = \frac{3}{4}$ ... the GCD of 3 and 4 is 1 ... $\frac{3}{4}$ is called the **simplest form** of the fractions equivalent to $0{\cdot}75$.

- We create equivalent forms by dividing numerator (top) and denominator (bottom) by the same number.

- We find the simplest form by dividing numerator and denominator by their GCD.

- We turn a decimal into a common fraction by remembering the meaning of the decimal ... $0{\cdot}75$ means 7 tenths and 5 hundredths or 75 hundredths:

  $$0{\cdot}75 = \frac{75}{100} = \frac{25 \times 3}{25 \times 4} = \frac{3}{4}$$

- While the denominator is 100, we often use a shorthand, called a percentage:

  $$\frac{3}{4} = 0{\cdot}75 = \frac{75}{100} = 75\%$$

- We find a fraction of a quantity by **multiplication**.

## EXAMPLE

Find $\frac{3}{4}$ of 80.

**Response**

$\frac{3}{4} = 3 \div 4$ so we get $80 \times 3 \div 4$ ... multiply by 3 and divide by 4.

**Using a calculator** this works well ... $80 \times 0{\cdot}75 = 60$

**Without a calculator**, we can choose to divide the 80 by 4 and then do the multiplication:

$80 \div 4 \times 3 = 20 \times 3 = 60$.

## MIXED NUMBERS

The number $5\frac{3}{4}$ is made up of the whole number 5 added to the fraction $\frac{3}{4}$

For that reason it is referred to as a **mixed number**.

Since 5 is equivalent to $\frac{20}{4}$ then $5\frac{3}{4}$ is equivalent to $\frac{23}{4}$.

Also, $23 \div 4 = 5{\cdot}75 \ldots 5\frac{3}{4} = 5{\cdot}75$.

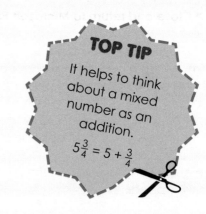

**TOP TIP**

It helps to think about a mixed number as an addition.

$5\frac{3}{4} = 5 + \frac{3}{4}$

20

## BE ACTIVE

## QUICK TESTS

1. Express two-fifths as:
   (a) a common fraction  (b) a decimal fraction  (c) a percentage

2. Find $\frac{3}{5}$ of 65

## QUICK TASKS

- Share a cake ...

  You have a square cake to share between three people.

  You find it very easy to halve things.

  So it should be no bother to quarter a square cake.

  Give each person a quarter ... leaving a quarter to share.

  Quarter the quarter and share it out again ... leaving a quarter of a quarter to share.

  Continue in this way so that each person gets a quarter plus a quarter of a quarter plus a quarter of a quarter of a quarter ...

  Explore the value of $\frac{1}{4} + (\frac{1}{4} \times \frac{1}{4}) + (\frac{1}{4} \times \frac{1}{4} \times \frac{1}{4}) + ...$ using your calculator.

- Farey Lights

  (a) Pick a number, e.g. 4

  (b) Write down all the fractions which have 4 or less as a denominator.

  $$\frac{0}{1} \ \frac{1}{1} \ \frac{0}{2} \ \frac{1}{2} \ \frac{2}{2} \ \frac{0}{3} \ \frac{1}{3} \ \frac{2}{3} \ \frac{3}{3} \ \frac{0}{4} \ \frac{1}{4} \ \frac{2}{4} \ \frac{3}{4} \ \frac{4}{4}$$

  (c) Simplify and put in order of size, ignoring duplicates.

  $$\frac{0}{1} \ \frac{1}{4} \ \frac{1}{3} \ \frac{1}{2} \ \frac{2}{3} \ \frac{3}{4} \ \frac{1}{1}$$

  This is called a Farey sequence.

  (d) Pick any three neighbouring terms in the sequence, e.g. $\frac{1}{2} \ \frac{2}{3} \ \frac{3}{4}$

  The fraction made by adding the numerators and denominators of the 'outside' pair will be equal to the fraction in the middle.

  $$\frac{1+3}{2+4} = \frac{4}{6} = \frac{2}{3}$$

  (e) Experiment.

# NUMBER, MEASURE AND MONEY

## MAKE THE LINK

- **Physics** – resistances in parallel require the use of fractions ...

  $$\frac{1}{R} = \frac{1}{R_1} + \frac{1}{R_2}$$

- **History** – the Egyptians only worked with fractions with unit numerator. Every other fractional amount had to be made of similar fractions e.g. $\frac{5}{6} = \frac{1}{2} + \frac{1}{3}$

  The Rhind Papyrus (1600 BC) discusses how to double such fractions and still express them as fractions with unit numerator e.g. $\frac{2}{9} = \frac{1}{5} + \frac{1}{45}$

## DID YOU KNOW?

Just as % means 'per cent' (... parts per 100)

5% of 60 = 60 × 5 ÷ 100 = 3

then ‰ means 'per mille' (... parts per 1000)

5‰ of 60 = 60 × 5 ÷ 1000 = 0·3

## OUR EVERYDAY LIVES:

During the credit crunch an employer asked his workforce to take a 10% pay decrease this year. He said he would make it up to them by giving them a 10% increase next year. Explore what happens.

**Response**

Look at what happens to £100 wage.

10% decrease: 10% of £100 = £10 ... New wage ... £100 – 10 = £90.

10% increase: 10% of £90 = £9 ... New wage ... £90 + 9 = £99

Each employee loses out by £1 for every £100 in their original wage.

# FRACTIONS, DECIMALS AND PERCENTAGES

## MULTIPLY COMMON FRACTIONS

This square has a side of 1 unit.
It has been split into fifths horizontally
and sixths vertically.
This divides the shape into 30ths.

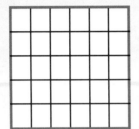

The area of a rectangle = length × breadth

So the shaded area below is $\frac{3}{5} \times \frac{5}{6}$

We can see that $\frac{3}{5} \times \frac{5}{6} = \frac{15}{30}$

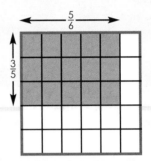

**To multiply fractions we multiply the numerators and multiply the denominators.**

### EXAMPLE

Calculate $\frac{2}{7} \times \frac{3}{4}$

**Response**

$\frac{2}{7} \times \frac{3}{4} = \frac{2 \times 3}{7 \times 4} = \frac{6}{28}$

We can simplify this by dividing by the GCD of 6 and 28, i.e. 2, to get $\frac{3}{14}$

## DIVIDE COMMON FRACTIONS

• The **reciprocal** of a number is what you multiply
  it by to make 1.

  The reciprocal of 2 is $\frac{1}{2}$ ... because $2 \times \frac{1}{2} = 1$

  The reciprocal of $\frac{3}{4}$ is $\frac{4}{3}$ ... because $\frac{3}{4} \times \frac{4}{3} = \frac{12}{12} = 1$

• **To divide by a number, we can multiply by its
  reciprocal.**

  **Example**    $16 \div 2$

  **Response**    $16 \div 2 = 16 \times \frac{1}{2} = \frac{16}{2} = 8$

• **To multiply and divide mixed numbers**

  When we wish to multiply or divide mixed
  numbers we should first turn them into top-
  heavy fractions.

  **Example**    Calculate $3\frac{2}{7} \times 2\frac{3}{4}$

  **Response**    $3\frac{2}{7} \times 2\frac{3}{4} = \frac{23}{7} \times \frac{11}{4} = \frac{23 \times 11}{7 \times 4} = \frac{253}{28} = 9\frac{1}{28}$

253 ÷ 28 = 9 remainder 1

22

## BE ACTIVE

### QUICK TESTS

1. Calculate:

   (a) $\frac{3}{5} \times \frac{2}{7}$ (b) $\frac{5}{9} \div \frac{2}{3}$

2. Calculate:

   (a) $2\frac{1}{4} \times 3\frac{2}{3}$ (b) $5\frac{1}{4} \div 3\frac{1}{2}$

### QUICK TASKS

• Why was the number 60 used when it came to subdividing the hour?

Find $\frac{1}{2}$ of 60; $\frac{1}{3}$ of 60; $\frac{1}{4}$ of 60; and so on.

Make a list of the fractions which give whole number answers.

Find $\frac{1}{2}$ of 10; $\frac{1}{3}$ of 100; $\frac{1}{4}$ of 100; and so on.

Make a list of the fractions which give whole number answers.

Remember that the calculator was not invented when they decided that 60 minutes make an hour. Why was the number 60 used?

## MAKE THE LINK

• **Mathematics** – the chances that some particular event will occur is usually expressed as a fraction.

• **Geography** – when making comparisons of all kinds, the geographer will use fractions: $\frac{3}{4}$ of the planet is covered with water; only 2·5% of the water is fresh; $\frac{1}{7}$ of an iceberg is above water. Probabilities are used in predicting the weather.

## DID YOU KNOW?

Speed (miles per hour) is calculated by dividing the distance (miles) by the time (hours). You can use your knowledge of fractions, decimals and percentages to work out speed. For example, what speed is a person walking at if he covers half a mile in three quarters of an hour?

**Response**

distance ÷ time = $\frac{1}{2} \div \frac{3}{4} = \frac{1}{2} \times \frac{4}{3} = \frac{1 \times 4}{2 \times 3} = \frac{4}{6} = \frac{2}{3}$

The person is walking at $\frac{2}{3}$ of a mile per hour.

23

## OUR EVERYDAY LIVES:

Many people make the mistake of adding numerators and denominators when asked to add fractions. They are actually finding the 'mediant'. It is still useful. It is a fraction which lies between the original two.

# ADD AND SUBTRACT FRACTIONS

## ADDING FRACTIONS

What is $\frac{1}{3} + \frac{3}{5}$?

Written out in words, we can see why it is not just a case of adding the 'bits'.

**What is one third plus three fifths?**

… we're trying to add together different things … thirds and fifths.

We can fix that using equivalent fractions

… thirds and fifths can both easily be turned into fifteenths.

$$\frac{1}{3} + \frac{3}{5} = \frac{1 \times 5}{3 \times 5} + \frac{3 \times 3}{5 \times 3} = \frac{5}{15} + \frac{9}{15} = \frac{14}{15}$$

Why did we choose fifteenths? 15 is a multiple of both 3 and 5.

In fact, the LCM of 3 and 5 is 15.

**EXAMPLE**

Evaluate $\frac{3}{10} + \frac{7}{15}$

**Response**

(Note that the LCM of 10 and 15 is 30)

$$\frac{3}{10} + \frac{7}{15}$$

$$= \frac{3 \times 3}{10 \times 3} + \frac{7 \times 2}{15 \times 2}$$

$$= \frac{9}{30} + \frac{14}{30}$$

$$= \frac{23}{30}$$

## SUBTRACTING FRACTIONS

The same technique is used to subtract fractions.

**Example**

Evaluate $\frac{7}{9} - \frac{5}{12}$

**Response**

(Note that the LCM of 9 and 12 is 36)

$$\frac{7}{9} - \frac{5}{12}$$

$$= \frac{7 \times 4}{9 \times 4} - \frac{5 \times 3}{12 \times 3}$$

$$= \frac{28}{36} - \frac{15}{36}$$

$$= \frac{13}{36}$$

## MIXED NUMBERS

**EXAMPLE 1**

Calculate $2\frac{2}{3} + 1\frac{1}{4}$.

**Response**

Think of it as: 2 and $\frac{2}{3}$ plus 1 and $\frac{1}{4}$

$$2 + \frac{2}{3} + 1 + \frac{1}{4} = 2 + 1 + \frac{2}{3} + \frac{1}{4} = 3 + \frac{8}{12} + \frac{3}{12} = 3\frac{11}{12}$$

**EXAMPLE 2**

Calculate $2\frac{2}{3} - 1\frac{1}{4}$.

**Response**

Think of it as: 2 and $\frac{2}{3}$ minus 1 minus $\frac{1}{4}$

$$2 + \frac{2}{3} - 1 - \frac{1}{4} = 2 - 1 + \frac{2}{3} - \frac{1}{4} = 1 + \frac{8}{12} - \frac{3}{12} = 1\frac{5}{12}$$

## BE ACTIVE

## QUICK TESTS

1. Find the sum $\frac{2}{7} + \frac{1}{4}$

2. Subtract $\frac{2}{5}$ from $\frac{3}{4}$

3. Calculate:
   (a) $3\frac{3}{5} + 1\frac{1}{6}$ (b) $3\frac{3}{5} - 1\frac{1}{6}$

4. Two rival football teams, United and Rovers, examined their stats.

   In the first half of the season they compared their performance.
   United had won 11 out of a possible 14 games; Rovers had won 16 out of 21 games.

   United are doing better. They have won $\frac{11}{14}$ of their games whereas Rovers have only won $\frac{16}{21}$.

   (a) Turn both fractions into decimals to check that United did indeed do better in the first half of the season.

   (b) In the second half of the season United won 11 out of a possible 22 games; Rovers won 7 out of 15 games.

   Check that United did better in the second half of the season too.

   (c) Altogether you can see that United won 22 out of 36 games and Rovers won 23 out of 36 games.

   How can United do better in both halves of the season yet do worse over the whole season?

# NUMBER, MEASURE AND MONEY

## MAKE THE LINK

- **Home Economics** – fractions are used in measuring. Sets of standard cups can be bought, or standard spoons, using fractions such as $\frac{1}{2}, \frac{1}{3}, \frac{1}{4}, \frac{1}{8}, \frac{1}{16}$.

  Look up some recipe books and see the regular occurrence of fractions.

## DID YOU KNOW?

Once upon a time a horse breeder had three sons. When he died he left half of his stock to the eldest son; a third to the middle son and a ninth to the youngest son.
There were 17 horses in the stock. So the eldest son was due $8\frac{1}{6}$ horses, the middle son $5\frac{2}{3}$ horses and the youngest son $1\frac{8}{9}$ horses.
Not wanting to butcher any horses, they consulted a wise man. He arrived with his horse and added it into the herd, making 18 horses in all.
The oldest son gets 9 horses (a half of 18), which is more than he was due, so he was happy;
The middle son gets 6 horses, which is more than he was due, so he was happy;
The youngest son gets 2 horses, which is more than he was due, so he was happy.
Now 9 + 6 + 2 = 17 horses … leaving one horse, the wise man's horse. The wise man rode off leaving everyone with more than they were due.
How is this possible?!

## OUR EVERYDAY LIVES:

The following picture was taken near Lindisfarne.

(a) How far is it between Chatton and Wooler?

(b) How far apart are Chatton and Belford?

**Response**
(a) From Chatton to Wooler = $3\frac{3}{4} + 3\frac{1}{2}$

$= 3 + 3 + \frac{3}{4} + \frac{1}{2} = 6 + \frac{3}{4} + \frac{2}{4} = 6\frac{5}{4} = 7\frac{1}{4}$ miles

(b) From Chatton to Belford = $6\frac{1}{2} - 3\frac{3}{4}$

$= 6 + \frac{1}{2} - 3 - \frac{3}{4} = 3 + \frac{2}{4} - \frac{3}{4} = 3 - \frac{1}{4} = 2\frac{3}{4}$ miles

# RATIO AND PROPORTION

## RATIO

A painter will mix tins of paint to get the colour he wants. When he mixes blue and yellow he gets green. The exact shade of green he gets depends on how much of each of the two basic colours he puts in the mix:

| yellow | 9:1 | 8:2 | 7:3 | 6:4 | 5:5 | 4:6 | 3:7 | 2:8 | 1:9 | blue |

Each colour has a different ratio of yellow:blue.

- Notice that 2:8 produces a different colour to 8:2.

  The order of the numbers in the ratio is important.

- Notice 2:8 means 2 parts yellow to 8 parts blue. This could also have been written:

  1 part yellow to 4 parts blue. 1:4 is a simplified version of 2:8.

They both produce the same colour.

If the first picture produces 5 litres of the colour then the second will produce 10 litres of the same colour.

### EXAMPLE

You can get another form of a ratio by multiplying both sides of the ratio by the same number.

**Example 1:** 2:8 = (2 × 3):(8 × 3) = 6:24

The painter can work this argument backwards to plan his mix.

**Example 2:** The painter wants to mix yellow and blue paint in the ratio 1:4 to get 30 litres of a special colour. How does he do it?

**Response**

1 part yellow and 4 parts blue means 5 parts altogether.

5 parts will make 30 litres if 1 part is 30 ÷ 5 = 6 litres.

If 1 part is 6 litres then 4 parts are 4 × 6 = 24 litres.

The painter needs 6 litres of yellow and 24 litres of blue.

## E ACTIVE

## QUICK TESTS

1. Share £44·80 between two people in the ratio 2:5.

2. Here is a pallette showing the different mixes of yellow and red.

   Express each ratio in its simplest form

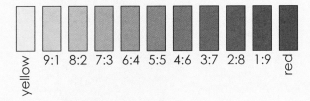

yellow 9:1 8:2 7:3 6:4 5:5 4:6 3:7 2:8 1:9 red

3. Simplify the ratio 154:231

## QUICK TASKS

- Make your own pallette of colours using Microsoft Word drawing tools:

  (i) Draw eleven rectangles

  (ii) Double Click the first one and choose 'Colors and lines' from the pop-up menu.

  (iii) Click to see all the colours and choose 'More colors...'

  (iv) Select colour sliders and choose CMYK sliders.

  These let you play with the mix of cyan(blue), magenta(red) and yellow.

  (v) Make magenta 100% and the rest 0%. Click OK, OK and the first box is red.

  (vi) Repeat the procedure with the 2nd box but make magenta 90% and cyan 10% with the others 0%.

  (vii) Continue dropping magenta and increasing the cyan by 10% till you get to the last box which is 100% cyan.

  (viii) You can make it like a spectrum by making all the boxes touching and choosing 'no line' from the drawing menu.

# NUMBER, MEASURE AND MONEY

## MAKE THE LINK

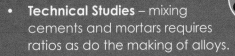

- **Technical Studies** – mixing cements and mortars requires ratios as do the making of alloys.

- **Physics** – in the study of machines the ratio of input force:output force is called the mechanical advantage of the machine and is a measure of how efficient the machine is.

- **History** – historians classify certain ages by the metalwork that the peoples could do. The Bronze Age is identified as the time when tools were made of bronze, which is a is a mix of tin and copper in the ratio tin:copper = 3:22 (12%:88%).

## DID YOU KNOW?

- One of the most famous ratios is called the golden ratio. Google 'Golden Ratio' and see how many amazing facts you can find out about it.

- Did you know that no matter how big you draw a circle, the ratio of the distance round it (the circumference) to the distance across it is fixed. Find out what you can about this ratio. It will become very important in your mathematical career.

## OUR EVERYDAY LIVES:

Ratios are needed to make sense of the gears on a bicycle. If the gear wheel at the pedal has 20 teeth and the gear wheel at the back wheel has 30 then the pedal has to turn 3 times to get the road-wheel to turn twice. This is expressed as the ratio 3:2.

# RATIO AND PROPORTION

## SIMPLE PROPORTIONAL PROBLEMS

There are two basic types of problems you can be asked to consider.

(a) Direct proportion: As one quantity **increases**, another **increases** in proportion.

(b) Inverse proportion: As one quantity **increases**, another **decreases** in proportion.

You should use your common sense to decide on your strategy.

**TOP TIP**
Use your common sense in problems of proportion.

### EXAMPLE 1: DIRECT PROPORTION

Getting to school, Bryan's total bus fare for the week (5 days) is £4·80.
How much will he spend in a week when Monday is a holiday?

**Response**
We are given that 5 days costs £4·80

So 1 day will be £4·80 ÷ 5 = £0·96. (Common sense … 1 day will cost $\frac{1}{5}$ of 5 days.)

So 4 days will be £0·96 × 4 = £3·84.

### EXAMPLE 2: INVERSE PROPORTION

The litter in the playground will take 4 men 51 minutes to clear up.
How quickly will the job be done by 6 men?

**Response**
We are given that 4 men take 51 minutes.

So 1 man will take 51 × 4 = 204 minutes.
(Common sense … 1 man will take 4 times as long as 4 men.)

So 6 men will take 204 ÷ 6 = 34 minutes.
(Common sense … 6 men will take $\frac{1}{6}$ of the time that 1 man takes.)

### EXAMPLE 3: NOT PROPORTION

Be careful when dealing with practical problems in this field.

Sometimes you can be fooled into making silly mistakes because, without thinking, the problem is treated as a proportional problem but the practicalities would rule the solution out.

Suppose a valeting service says that it takes 2 people 20 minutes to clean the inside of a car.

One could imagine that 1 person would take twice as long … fair enough. But what about putting 20 people on the job?

Would they take 2 minutes?

(By the way, the record for getting people in a Smart car stands at 14.)

28

**E ACTIVE**

## UICK TESTS

1. A garden centre makes potting compost by mixing loam, peat and sand in the ratio loam:peat:sand = 7:3:2.

   They sell the compost in 60-litre bags.

   How much of each ingredient do they need for a bag?

2. The same centre will make up compost for heathers. This can come in 30-litre or 50-litre bags.

   In the 30-litre bags there are 12 **potfuls** of loam, 15 **potfuls** of peat and 6 **potfuls** of sand.

   How would they make up the 50-litre bag?

## UICK TASKS

* This recipe for tablet serves 6 people. Adjust it to make tablet for 4 people.

  6 cups of sugar
  180 g of butter
  612 g condensed milk
  510 ml water

# NUMBER, MEASURE AND MONEY

## MAKE THE LINK

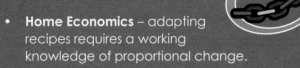

* **Home Economics** – adapting recipes requires a working knowledge of proportional change.

* **History** – organic artefacts can be dated by measuring the proportion of carbon 14 they contain compared to carbon 12.

* **Music** – musical instruments, particularly percussion instruments, depend on paying attention to the alloys used, e.g. a pair of cymbals are typically made from a bronze which is tin:copper = 1:4. Raising the proportion of tin lowers the pitch of the cymbal.

* **Geography** – land use and forestry management both make a lot of use of ratio and proportion in their statistics.

## DID YOU KNOW?

29

The chemistry department uses direct proportion to calculate how much water to add when diluting acid to a known strength, e.g. a 30% solution of acid means 30% is acid and 70% is water. How much water must be added to 4 litres of concentrated acid to make it a 30% solution?

## OUR EVERYDAY LIVES:

On many occasions, especially when dealing with portions or fair division of materials, the proportions are important. If you increase the number of rooms that must be painted then you'll increase the amount of the paint mix you'll need, but the proportions of yellow and blue should be kept the same.

The same idea applies when you alter recipes to cater for a different number of people from what the recipe was written for.

## MONEY

### INTEREST

In 1970 your granddad could buy a can of juice for 10p. Nowadays he would have to pay £1.

Does that mean your granddad could buy ten times as much then as he can now?

Not at all. In 1970 it took just as long to earn enough to buy a can of juice as it does now. The buying power of money gets less as time goes by.

If people thought about putting £1 in a bank when it could buy 10 cans and then taking it out to spend when it can only buy one, they would never leave money in the bank. They would spend it while its buying power was high.

To get round this, banks offer **interest** that allows money to 'grow' as it sits in the deposit account.

### EXAMPLE

A bank might offer 6% interest a year.
6% of £5 = 5 × 0·06 = £0·30
That means that if you leave £5 in the bank for a year, you'll find that there is £5·30 after a year.
Another way of thinking about it: if you start with 100% then after a year there will be 106%.
If you put £5 in the bank, then after a year this would be 106% of £5 = 5 × 1·06 =£5·30.

What if you leave it for a second year?
106% of £5·30 = 5·30 × 1·06 = £5·62 (to the nearest penny).
As each year passes you multiply by another factor of 1·06.
(Of course, you shouldn't round off till the end of the problem.)

To deal with this properly, you will need a calculator.
You can get the calculator to behave like your bank account.
Step 1 Put £5 in the bank ... type 5 and then =.
Step 2 Now let a year pass ... type ×1·06 =
Step 3 Let another year pass ... type =
Thereafter each time you press = another year passes.
How many times must you press it before the £5 has grown to £50?
After 40 pushes (years) it has grown to £51·43.

That's good. If your granddad had put £5 in the bank in 1970 at 6% interest a year then it would be worth ten times as much now. The buying power of your granddad's fiver is still the same.

Of course the same idea applies when you borrow money.

### APR

Often, especially when you are borrowing money, the rate of interest is given monthly ... it looks quite small. The annual percentage rate (APR) can be calculated to give you a guide for the sake of comparison with other deals.

### EXAMPLE

A loan company offers money at a monthly rate of 1·6%.
What is the APR?

**Response**
For the sake of convenience consider a loan of £100 borrowed for 12 months.

Each month the money grows by a factor of 1·016
100 × 1·016 × 1·016 ... **12 factors** ... × 1·016 × 1·016 = 120·98
After a year, for every £100 the borrower pays £20·98.
This translates as 20·98% per annum.
Quite a high rate.

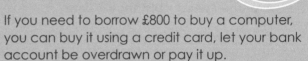

## BE ACTIVE

## QUICK TESTS

1. Calculate the interest when £650 is put in the bank for 4 years at 4% p.a.

2. What is the cost of a loan of £4500 for 3 years when the rate of interest is 6·5% p.a.?

3. What is the equivalent APR to a monthly rate of 1·25%?

4. Which is the best deal if you want to borrow £500

   (i) a rate of 1·3% per month  (ii) an APR of 17%  (iii) pay £48 monthly for 12 months?

## QUICK TASKS

- Do an internet search to discover current rates on

  (i) credit cards  (ii) banks  (iii) hire purchase terms (paying up).

  These rates change on a regular basis.

- Compare the rates from before and after the 'Credit Crunch'.

- See if you can set up a spreadsheet to convert monthly rates to APR and vice versa.

- In October of 2008 a leading store offered its own credit card as one solution to parents who did not have the cash to buy presents for their children in the run-up to Christmas. You could borrow £100, then pay it back at £5 a week for 27 weeks. You would pay back £135 to borrow £100. What is the APR?

  Make a spreadsheet to work this out.

  (i) In A1 type WEEK; in B1 type INTEREST; in C1 BALANCE; in D1 RATE%

  (ii) In C2 type 100; in D2 type 1

  (iii) In A3 type 1; in B3 type = C2*$D$2/100; in C3 type =C2+B3-5.

  (iv) Fill row 3 down to row 29 to show week 27 (A29 should read 27.)

  (v) Experiment with different values in D2 (the weekly rate of interest). You're looking for the figure that will make the balance less than 50p in week 27.

  (vi) In C31 type =100*(1+D2/100)^52-100 which will turn the weekly rate into the APR.

# NUMBER, MEASURE AND MONEY

## MAKE THE LINK

- **Business Studies** – loans and interest form a major part of this course.

- **History** – compare the buying power of money say, during WWII with today.

  The failure of the Darien Venture lead directly to the Union of Parliaments.

  The South Sea Bubble has echoes of the credit crunch.

- **Geography** – comparative studies of the economies of different nations affect trade and commerce.

## DID YOU KNOW?

If you need to borrow £800 to buy a computer, you can buy it using a credit card, let your bank account be overdrawn or pay it up.

You should always convert them all to the same thing, e.g. APR or total cost, before making up your mind, and it's always worth comparing deals. For example, a credit card offers an interest rate of 1·36% a month; your bank charges 19·5% APR for an overdraft; the shop will allow you to make 12 monthly instalments of £79.

Which is offering the best rate?

31

## OUR EVERYDAY LIVES:

Although all of this topic is by its nature practical we should be aware that other considerations apart from the best APR might shape our decision-making.

In the current 'Credit Crunch' you may find lenders reluctant to lend all the money.

They may only be prepared to lend, say, 90%, leaving you to find 10% straight away.

You may find that a 'paying-up' scheme is dependent on your taking out some sort of extra guarantee or insurance.

# TIME, DISTANCE, SPEED

## AVERAGE SPEED

The distance between Glasgow and Galashiels is 76·5 miles.

Last week I made the journey. It was slow-going on the country roads, but when I got to the motorway I made good progress, except for the bit of roadworks at Harthill.

The whole journey took me one and a half hours.

Although I varied my speed, I covered 76·5 miles in 1·5 hours …

76·5 ÷ 1·5 = 51

I travelled at an **average** speed of 51 miles per hour.

**Average Speed = Distance ÷ Time**

Note that the distance was measured in miles, the time in hours and therefore the final speed is measured in miles per hour.

## EXAMPLE

In 1954 Roger Bannister was the first man to run the mile in under 4 minutes. What was the average speed that he ran the mile (in miles per hour)?

**Response**

4 minutes = 4 ÷ 60 hours = 0·06666… hours

Speed = 1 ÷ 0·06666… = 15 miles per hour.

## CALCULATING DISTANCE 1

The cheetah is fast! It can run at 70 mph for 3 minutes.

What distance does it cover in this time?

3 minutes = (3 ÷ 60) hours = 0·05 hours

The distance the cheetah covers = 70 × 0·05 = 3·5 miles.

The units depend on the context.

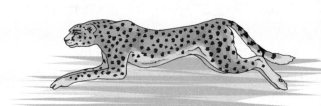

## UICK TESTS

1. The Grand National is a famous horse race. It is 7242 m long.

   The quickest time was set in 1990 at 8·8 minutes.

   At what average speed did the winner run the race?

## UICK TASKS

- When the Winter Olympics come round, get enough data so that you can work out average speeds for the downhill racers, for the luge and for the speed skating.

  Write a report on the comparison.

- Go to Multimap or the AA routefinder and ask for directions for some journey you make often. Get a print-out and see what average speeds they assume.

# NUMBER, MEASURE AND MONEY

## MAKE THE LINK

- **History** – 'Forced marches' feature largely in Caesar's Gallic wars and the like. A forced march was 25 miles a day instead of the standard 15. Arriving before the enemy expected you was desirable.

## DID YOU KNOW?

Most people remember what to do when handling speed, distance, time problems by remembering this triangle:

You cover up the letter you want in order to find the corresponding formula:

Covering S we find: $S = \frac{D}{T}$ ($S = D \div T$)

33

## OUR EVERYDAY LIVES:

Knowing how to work out speed, distance and time can help us to plan journeys. For example, on a trip from my house to the Ardrossan pier (108 miles) to catch a ferry, I know from experience that I can average 50 miles per hour. The ferry leaves at 12 30 pm but I have to check in half-an-hour before that.

(a) When should I leave the house?

(b) Using a route-finder on the internet I find the route described as 108 miles, 2h 24 min. What average speed are they assuming?

**Response**

(a) Time = Distance ÷ Speed
   Time = 108 ÷ 50 = 2·16 = 2h 10 min to the nearest minute [0·16 × 60 = 9·6]

   Working backwards:
   The ferry leaves at 12 30. So I have to be there at 12 noon.
   I should leave at 9 50 a.m. to catch the ferry.

(b) 2h 24 min = 2 + (24 ÷ 60) = 2·4 hours
   Speed = Distance ÷ time
   Speed = 108 ÷ 2·4 = 45 miles per hour.

# TIME, DISTANCE, SPEED

## CALCULATING DISTANCE 2

Given that Speed = Distance ÷ Time
it follows that

**Distance = Speed × Time**
(Think: if 5 = 20 ÷ 4 then 20 = 5 × 4.)

We still have to be careful with units …

The speed is given in **miles per hour** so we should
measure time in **hours** and get our distance in **miles**.

### EXAMPLE

Light travels at 299 800 km per second.

A laser beam is bounced off the Moon. The time it takes it to get to the Moon and back is 2·57 seconds.

How far away is the Moon? (Remember that the distance travelled by the beam is to the Moon and back.)

Give your answer correct to 3 significant figures.

### Response

Check the units … kilometres and seconds.

Distance travelled = Speed × Time = 299 800 × 2·57 = 770 486 km

Distance to Moon = 770 486 ÷ 2 = 385 000 km (to 3 s.f.)

## CALCULATING TIME TAKEN

Given that Distance = Speed × Time.
it follows that

**Time = Distance ÷ Speed**
(Think: If 20 = 4 × 5 then 5 = 20 ÷ 4)

When working with time, we should turn the decimal part of an hour into minutes by multiplying by 60 and the decimal part of a minute into seconds also by multiplying by 60.

### EXAMPLE

In the 18th century, so the story goes, Dick Turpin rode the distance between London and York, a distance of 200 miles, at a gallop of 14 miles per hour. At the end of the journey his poor horse, Black Bess, dropped dead.

If these figures are taken as accurate, work out, to the nearest minute, how long the journey took him.

### Response

Time = Distance ÷ Speed

Time = 200 ÷ 14 = 14·2857… [14 hours]

0·2857… × 60 = 17·1428… [17 minutes]

He took 14 hours and 17 minutes to make the journey.

## BE ACTIVE

### QUICK TESTS

1. The earth travels round the Sun at a speed of 2 570 000 km per day.

   It takes 365·25 days to go round the Sun.

   What is the distance the Earth travels in one orbit of the Sun?

2. The bobsleigh run is 1200 m long. A four-man team completed the run at an average speed of 110 km/hr.

   Calculate their time to the nearest hundredth of a second.

### QUICK TASKS

- Look up the highway code and see what they consider to be the stopping distances for different speeds.

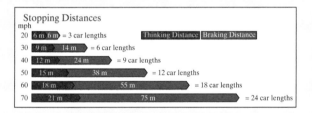

Stopping Distances

| mph | | |
|---|---|---|
| 20 | 6 m / 6 m = 3 car lengths | Thinking Distance / Braking Distance |
| 30 | 9 m / 14 m = 6 car lengths | |
| 40 | 12 m / 24 m = 9 car lengths | |
| 50 | 15 m / 38 m = 12 car lengths | |
| 60 | 18 m / 55 m = 18 car lengths | |
| 70 | 21 m / 75 m = 24 car lengths | |

Look particularly at the 'Thinking Distance'. If your reaction time is 0·2 of a second, how far will you have travelled if you are going at 32 km/h? Remember this is the time before you even start to apply the brakes.

Make a table of reaction time versus speed. If talking on the phone makes your reaction time slower by 1 second, what effect does this have on the thinking distance?

## MAKE THE LINK

- **Physics** – Galileo and Newton did experimentation on motion. Both derived formulae which deal with speed, distance and time (though speed is handled as a quantity which has size and direction).

  The speed of light and the speed of sound are studied. Measuring these speeds takes a lot of ingenuity.

- **Geography** – for a whole new feel for units, continental drift makes the speed of a glacier sound fast. Famous fault-lines like the San Andreas fault in California can be studied to explain earthquakes.

  The Pacific plate is moving at a speed of 2 cm per year. However, at the fault line there is not a continuous movement. At the moment it is estimated that about 8 m of movement have accumulated since the last large earthquake. When the fault releases there will be another.

## DID YOU KNOW?

Covering D we find: D = ST (D = S x T)

Covering T we find: $T = \dfrac{D}{S}$ (T = D ÷ S)

## OUR EVERYDAY LIVES:

On the road between Kilmarnock and Girvin there are 40 banks of cameras. These photograph the car and use software to read the registration number. They also imprint the time of day on the photo.

If a car goes between any two stations and its average speed works out more than the speed limit permits, the driver will be fined and get 3 penalty points on his or her licence.

# MEASUREMENT

## LENGTH 1

In the late 18th century there were 250 000 different units of weights and measurement in France.

In 1792 the French scientific community invented the metric system. They defined the metre as one ten-millionth of the distance from the North pole to the equator.

All the metric units of length, area, volume and weight are derived from this one measurement.

### EXAMPLE

| 1 kilometre | ... | 1000 metres | ... | a bit less than Princes St in Edinburgh |
| 1 metre | ... | 1 metre | ... | the distance from your nose to your fingertip |
| 1 decimetre | ... | $\frac{1}{10}$ metre | ... | the width of your hand including the thumb |
| 1 centimetre | ... | $\frac{1}{100}$ metre | ... | the width of your pinkie |
| 1 millimetre | ... | $\frac{1}{1000}$ metre | ... | the thickness of a coin |

There are many ways of measuring length including the ruler, tape measure and trundle wheel. More modern tools exploit the speed of light (laser distance finder), speed of sound (ultrasonic distance finder) or the focusing required by a lens (optical distance finder). We can also use the same GPS that's used to give directions. The user must be aware that each tool has a cost and also a degree of accuracy.

## PERIMETERS

The distance round a 2D shape is called its perimeter.

You find it for any shape with straight sides by adding the lengths.

- Sometimes you can deduce the lengths of sides.

### EXAMPLE 1

In a rectangle, opposite sides are equal. So from rectangle 1 we can figure out rectangle 2:

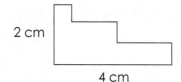

So the perimeter = 2 + 4 + 2 + 4 = 12 cm

- Sometimes you can't deduce individual sizes but you can deduce the total length of some sides.

### EXAMPLE 2

Although we cannot figure out the lengths of the individual bits that make up the stepped part, you should be able to see that all the horizontal parts add up to 4 cm and all the vertical parts add up to 2 cm.

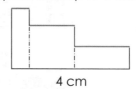

So once again the perimeter = 2 + 4 + 2 + 4 = 12 cm.

36

E ACTIVE

## QUICK TEST

1. A travelling salesman checks mileage on a route-finder on the internet.

| Route | Distance (miles) | Time |
|---|---|---|
| Glasgow to Stirling | 26·8 | 42 min |
| Stirling to Edinburgh | 36·1 | 57 min |
| Glasgow to Edinburgh | 46·3 | 1h 4 min |

(a) How many miles will be added to his journey from Glasgow to Edinburgh by going via Stirling?

(b) How much time will be added?

2. In 2004 a rare astronomical event occurred.

Venus moved between the Earth and the Sun (a transit of Venus). Venus is 108 million kilometres from the Sun. Earth is 149·6 million km from the Sun.

How far apart were Earth and Venus at the moment of transit?

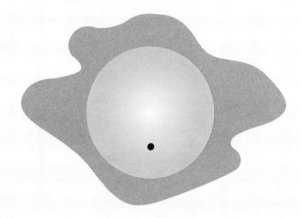

3. How thick is a piece of paper? A ream of paper (500 sheets) is measured as being 5 cm thick.

(a) How thick is one sheet?

(b) Suppose the original measurement for a ream was 1 mm out. What difference would this make to your answer?

4. A geographer will tell you that the line separating the Earth's crust and its mantle is known as the Moho (Mohorovičić discontinuity). Scientists are still trying to drill down to it.

A group of drillers tried in 2005. They drilled down 25 m each day for 8 weeks.

How far did they get, in kilometres correct to 1 decimal place?

5. Find the perimeter of each shape.

(a)

(b)
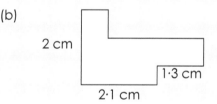

## QUICK TASKS

- Use the internet to prepare a presentation on the history of measurement of length.

  Noah was given instructions to build the ark. The measurements are given in cubits. Find out what a cubit is. In *Star Wars* they mention 'light years' and 'parsecs' as distances. Try and find out what these are.

- Find out how far it is from school to home by walking there and counting the number of steps. Experiment to find what your average pace is. Note how far you get in 100 paces and use a tape measure to measure this accurately.

  Use the internet and a route finder to find this distance accurately. Try to find reasons for the two answers being different.

# MEASUREMENT

### LENGTH 2

Sometimes problems involve circles.

It has been known since ancient times that the distance round a circle is roughly 3 times the distance across it.

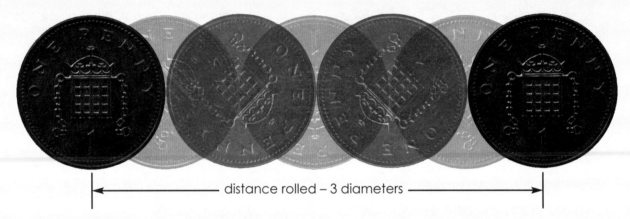

distance rolled – 3 diameters

A coin will roll a distance equal to three diameters.

This factor of 3 is just approximate. A better guide is 3·14.

The calculator gives an even better answer if you use the button marked π (pronounced pi).

The perimeter of a circle is called its circumference.

$$C = \pi D$$

---

**EXAMPLE**

A wheel has a diameter of 45 cm. How far will it roll in one turn?

**Response**

It will roll one circumference. $C = \pi D$ so $C = \pi \times 45 = 141$ cm to the nearest centimetre.

---

Sometimes you are dealing with a mixture of shapes.

---

**EXAMPLE**

Following the inside track of a racecourse a runner will follow a route shaped like a rectangle with a semicircle on each end. What's the length of one lap?

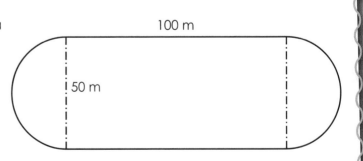

100 m

50 m

**Response**

The perimeter is made of two straights and 2 semicircles (a whole circle).

$P = (2 \times 100) + (\pi \times 50) = 200 + 157 = 357$ m (to nearest metre)

---

**E ACTIVE**

## QUICK TESTS

1. Find the perimeter of each shape.

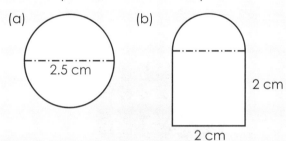

(a) 2.5 cm

(b) 2 cm / 2 cm

## QUICK TASKS

- How did the ancients discover π? Get several circular objects. Use string or a flexible tape to help you measure their circumferences. Measure their diameters.

- Make a table like this one:

| Object | Diameter | Circumference |
|---|---|---|
| Plate | 20 | 63 |
| Can | 8 | 25 |
| Coffee lid | 10 | 31 |
| Cheese box | 12 | 38 |
| Cup | 7 | 22 |
| Coin | 2 | 6 |

… and even a chart.

You should find that all the points lie in a straight line, passing through the origin. (If the diameter = 0 cm then the circumference will be 0 cm.)

This is an indication that the two things, diameter and circumference, are related.

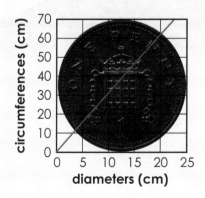

circumferences (cm) / diameters (cm)

# NUMBER, MEASURE AND MONEY

## MAKE THE LINK

- **IT** – Global positioning systems have revolutionised measuring.

- **Geography** – These skills are required for measuring distance on the globe; map reading and scale drawing.

- **Modern Studies** – Political decisions such as territorial limits are based on length. Most countries claim 12 nautical miles off their shoreline as part of their territory – one reason the UK lays a claim to Rockall.

## DID YOU KNOW?

In 1999 a £125 million dollar spacecraft crashed on Mars because of a mix-up in using imperial rather than metric units. The imperial system of measurement, which uses miles, yards, feet was replaced by the metric system in 1971 in the UK but is still used in the USA.

## OUR EVERYDAY LIVES:

### Example
A TV aerial comes in through the wall at one point in a room. It has to follow the skirting round the room to the position of the TV.

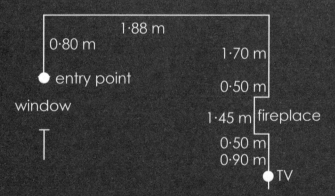

1·88 m
0·80 m
entry point
1·70 m
0·50 m
window
1·45 m  fireplace
0·50 m
0·90 m
TV

What total length of cable is needed?

### Response
0·80 + 1·88 + 1·70 + 0·50 + 1·45 + 0·50 + 0·90 = 7·73 m

You might lay out the problem in columns, keeping the decimal points in line.

Of course, being a real problem, you'll probably have to buy 8 m of cable at the shops.

## MEASUREMENT

### AREA 1

#### EXAMPLE

As an eco-friendly act, a householder wants to install solar panels. One panel is 4 m by 6 m and the other 3 m by 7 m. They are both priced the same. Which one would be better at capturing light?

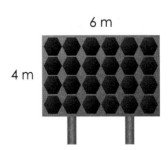

6 m

4 m

**Response**

The first panel is wider, the second is longer, both have the same perimeter.

However the first has 24 squares of side 1 metre to cover it and the second only has 21.

The first has the bigger 'surface', and should capture more light.

Because of problems such as this, we have had to find ways of calculating the areas of many shapes.

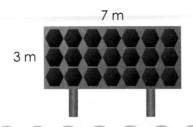

7 m

3 m

#### THE RECTANGLE

You should already know how to find the area of a rectangle:

$A = lb$ where $l$ is the length and $b$ is the breadth (both measured in the same units).

**Example:** A rectangle 6 m by 4 m has an area $A = 6 \times 4 = 24$ m$^2$

#### THE RIGHT-ANGLED TRIANGLE

We can see that the triangle opposite is half of the rectangle which has a length $b$ units and a breadth of $a$ units.

Talking about the triangle $b$ is the length of the base and $a$ is its height measured at right angles to the base ... its altitude.

The area of the rectangle is $ab$ units$^2$ and so $A = \frac{1}{2}ab$ gives the area of the right-angled triangle.

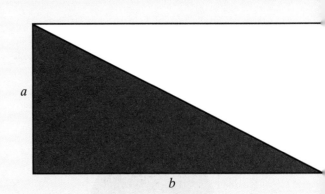

$a$

$b$

#### ANY TRIANGLE

Any triangle can be split into two right-angled triangles with a common altitude.

Area $= \frac{1}{2}ap + \frac{1}{2}aq = \frac{1}{2}a(p + q) = \frac{1}{2}ab$

$A = \frac{1}{2}ab$ gives the area of any triangle.

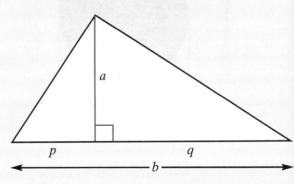

$a$

$p$     $q$

$b$

**BE ACTIVE**

## QUICK TESTS

1. Find the area of each shape.

   (a) a rectangle which has a length of 1·2 cm and breadth 3·6 cm.

   (b) a triangle which has a base of 8 cm and an altitude of 5 cm.

## QUICK TASKS

- Consider this set of shapes sitting on a grid.

  The area covered by the 4 coloured shapes is 32·5 squares.

  Check it out.

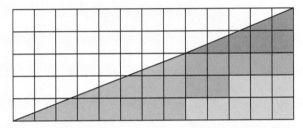

  Now swap round the green and blue triangles

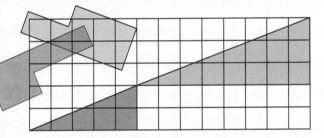

  and position the red and orange shapes to fit into the space that is left.

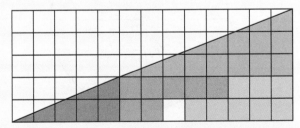

  Just where did that extra square come from?

  What have the Fibonacci numbers got to do with it?

  Make a set of these shapes as accurately as you can and explore the area paradox.

  Look up 'area paradox' on the internet.

# NUMBER, MEASURE AND MONEY

## MAKE THE LINK

- **English** – research could be done on the etymology of the names of the units, on euphemisms such as 'God's little acre' for a cemetery, 'the Square mile' for the City of London, the 'Square mile of murder' for an area of Glasgow, and the books which borrowed these expressions as titles.

## DID YOU KNOW?

It's hard to believe but these two triangles have the same area.

Can you prove it?

41

## OUR EVERYDAY LIVES:

When involved in DIY, you have to be careful with the practicalities in the problem.

When measuring up a rectangular floor to buy a carpet, you have to be careful to get 'too much' in both length and breadth so you can cut back and have a good fit.

If you are buying boxes of tiles to do a job, remember you can't buy half a box.

### Example
A tiler wants to cover a rectangular area in the kitchen with tiles.
The area is 262 cm by 143 cm. The tiles are 10 cm by 10 cm. They come in boxes of 20.
How many boxes should the tiler order?

Before doing the calculations you must realise that when you have to cut a tile to fit, the material cut off is waste and will not be usable elsewhere.

### Wrong response
Area to be covered: 262 × 143 = 37 466 cm²
Area of a tile: 10 × 10 = 100 cm²
Number of tiles needed: 37 466 ÷ 100 = 374·66 tiles ... 374 tiles
Number of boxes: 374 ÷ 20 = 18·7 ... 19 boxes.

**(See p.41 for correct response)**

# MEASUREMENT

### AREA 2

#### KITE AND RHOMBUS

Both can be thought of as being made of two congruent triangles placed back-to-back.

$$\text{Area} = 2 \times \tfrac{1}{2}d_1 p = 2 \times \tfrac{1}{2}d_1 \times \tfrac{1}{2}d_2 = \tfrac{1}{2}d_1 d_2$$

$A = \tfrac{1}{2}d_1 d_2$ gives the area of a kite or rhombus

where $d_1$ and $d_2$ are the diagonals.

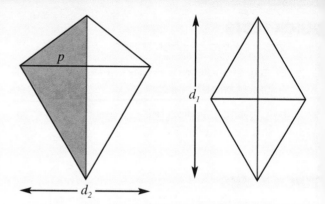

#### PARALLELOGRAM

Think of the parallelogram as two congruent triangles.

$$\text{Area} = 2 \times \tfrac{1}{2}bh = bh$$

$A = bh$ where $b$ is the base and $h$ is the perpendicular distance between the base and the opposite side.

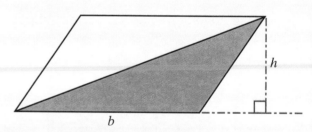

#### TRAPEZIUM

Think of the trapezium as two triangles which have a common altitude.

$$\text{Area} = \tfrac{1}{2}p_1 h + \tfrac{1}{2}p_2 h = \tfrac{1}{2}h(p_1 + p_2)$$

where $p_1$ and $p_2$ are the lengths of the parallels and $h$ is the distance between them.

For each of the shapes above, as long as you know how to find the area of a triangle, and can split the shape into the correct triangles, you don't need to learn a big list of formulae.

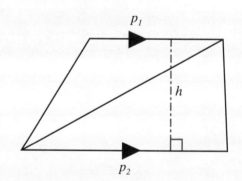

#### CIRCLE

Take a circle. Slice it into many segments as you would a pizza.

Now flip the segments so you can rejoin them to form a parallelogram-like shape.

The more slices you make, the more it looks like a parallelogram.

The area of the 'parallelogram' $= bh = \pi r \times r$

The area of a circle, $A = \pi r^2$ where $r$ is the radius.

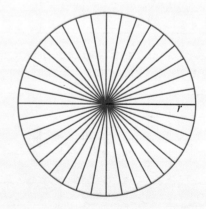

### UNITS

When you multiply one length by another make sure the units are the same.

The resultant area will be measured in the corresponding square units.

$\text{mm} \times \text{mm} = \text{mm}^2$; $\text{cm} \times \text{cm} = \text{cm}^2$; $\text{m} \times \text{m} = \text{m}^2$.

When finding the area of land, the numbers can get quite big, so more convenient units exist:

$100 \text{ m}^2 = 1$ are; $10\,000 \text{ m}^2 = 100$ ares $= 1$ hectare.

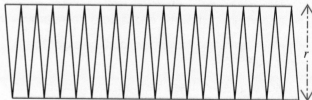

half the circumference of circle $= \pi r$

42

**E ACTIVE**

## QUICK TESTS

1. Find the area of each shape:

   (a) a rhombus whose diagonals are of length 3·2 m and 8·1 m

   (b) a kite whose diagonals are of length 3·2 mm and 8·1 mm

   (c) a parallelogram of base 5·5 km and corresponding altitude 9·0 km

   (d) a trapezium with parallel sides of length 12·5 cm and 7·8 cm which are 3·4 cm apart.

   (e) a circle of diameter 10 m.

# NUMBER, MEASURE AND MONEY

## MAKE THE LINK

- **History** – the Domesday Book records who owned land in the late part of the 11th century in England. The basic unit of land was the 'manor', which varied in size. These were part of larger areas called 'Hundreds'.

## DID YOU KNOW?

- Trappers and other people who have to work in regions with a lot of snow use snowshoes to get around. Explore how these work; what is their connection to the question 'Why do camels have big feet?'

43

## OUR EVERYDAY LIVES:

**Example** (continued from page 39)
**Correct response**
Consider the rectangle:
How many tiles are needed to make a row?
(Remember to round up. If you need a bit of a tile, you'll cut it from a whole tile.)
262 ÷ 10 = 26·2 tiles = 27 tiles.
How many rows need tiles?
(Remember again to round up. If you need a bit of a tile, you'll cut it from a whole tile.)
143 ÷ 10 = 14·3 rows = 15 rows.
How many tiles do you need?
27 × 15 = 405 tiles.
How many boxes do you need?
405 ÷ 20 = 20·25 boxes = 21 boxes.

By the wrong method you'll end up 2 boxes short.

# MEASUREMENT

## AREA 3

Complex shapes can often be broken down into groups of simple shapes.

### EXAMPLE 1

A farmer wishes to find the area of a plot of land, ABCD. He measures AC as 100 m. He measures the perpendicular distance from this line to B as 40 m and to D as 60 m. What is the area of the plot?

**Response**

Draw a sketch and enter the data:

Area = $\triangle$ABC + = $\triangle$ADC

$= \frac{1}{2} \times 100 \times 40 + \frac{1}{2} \times 100 \times 60$

$= 2000 + 3000 = 5000 \text{ m}^2$

$= 50$ ares

$= 0{\cdot}5$ hectares.

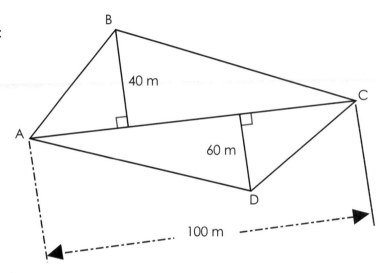

### EXAMPLE 2

In ancient Rome, the Romans held chariot races in a venue called the Circus Maximus. The diagram gives its approximate shape and size.

621 m

118 m

What area is enclosed in the Circus Maximus?

**Response**

Area = area of circle radius 59 m + area of rectangle which is 621 m by 118 m

$= \pi \times 59^2 + (621 \times 118)$

$= 10\,936 + 73\,278$ (to nearest whole number)

$= 84\,214 \text{ m}^2$

$= 8{\cdot}42$ hectares ( to 3 s.f.)

**TOP TIP**

If you can break a shape up into triangles, rectangles or bits of circles you can find its area as long as you have enough data.

44

**E ACTIVE**

## UICK TESTS

1. This label for a tin of beans is made up from two semicircles of radius 4 cm and 2 cm and a trapezium with parallel sides of length 15 cm and 8 cm which are 7 cm apart.

   Calculate its area.

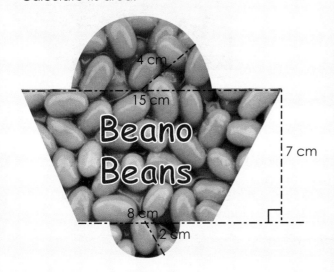

# NUMBER, MEASURE AND MONEY

## MAKE THE LINK

- **Science** – in science many things exhibit the inverse square law. If you increase the distance from a source of light by a factor of $x$, the intensity of light falls by a factor of $x^2$. The same phenomenon is encountered with sound, magnetism and gravity.

  Intensity is a measure of the amount of light falling on a particular area. If, for example, you double the distance, and consider a rectangle on which the light falls, it doubles its length and its breadth and so its area is 4 times bigger. The same light has to cover 4 times the area.

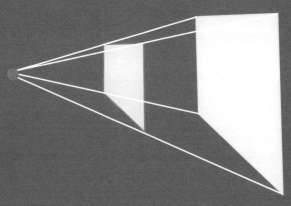

45

- **Geography** – an important statistic about a country or city is its population density. This is the number of people living in a fixed area usually a $km^2$. Population Density = Population ÷ Area

- **Sport** – the power generated by a sail on a yacht is a direct function of the area of the sail.

- **Space** – Kepler discovered that a planet as it orbits the Sun will sweep through equal areas in equal time. See A in diagram.

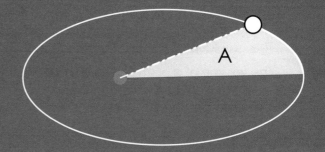

# MEASUREMENT

## VOLUME

The volume of an object is the amount of 3D space it occupies.

The volume of a cuboid is calculated by counting cubes. We can also multiply length by breadth to find how many cubes are in one layer, then multiply by height (the number of layers) to find the volume: $V = lbh$

In this example $V = 4 \times 3 \times 2 = 24$ cubic units

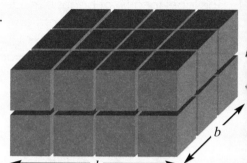

## UNITS

The basic unit of measurement of volume is the cubic unit.

### EXAMPLE

- A cubic millimetre, $mm^3$, is the about the volume of a grain of sugar.
- A cubic centimetre, $cm^3$, is the volume of a dice with side 1 cm.
- A cubic metre, $m^3$, is about the volume of a cosy armchair.
- A cubic kilometre, $km^3$, is about 1000 times the volume of the Empire State Building, or 100 times the amount of dirt shifted when making the Channel Tunnel.

For everyday groceries the cubic centimetre can be too small but the cubic metre can be too big. There are $100 \times 100 \times 100 = 1\,000\,000$ $cm^3$ in $1$ $m^3$.

For this reason an intermediate unit has been devised, the litre.
$1000$ $cm^3$ = 1 litre
$1000$ litres = $1$ $m^3$.

$\frac{1}{1000}$ of a litre is called a millilitre. Note that this is **exactly** the same as a cubic centimetre.
$1$ ml = $1$ $cm^3$

## PRISMS

A prism is a solid with constant cross-section. Many solids belong to this family.

Each takes its name from the type of base it has. The rectangular prism is usually called a cuboid. The circular prism is called a cylinder.

The volume of a prism = area of base × height
… where by **height** we mean the distance between the congruent ends.

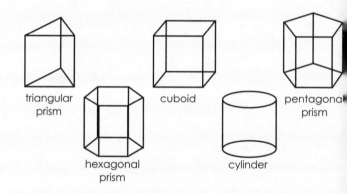

triangular prism          cuboid          pentagonal prism

hexagonal prism          cylinder

### Example 1

Calculate the volume of the sweetie box.

### Response

The box is a triangular prism.

V = Area of triangle × Height.

$V = \frac{1}{2} \times 4 \cdot 3 \times 5 \times 12$

$= 129$ $cm^3$

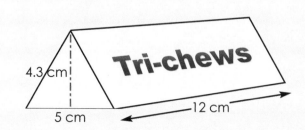

4.3 cm          **Tri-chews**

5 cm          12 cm

46

## QUICK TESTS

1. Find the volume of each shape.

(a)

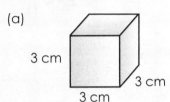

3 cm
3 cm
3 cm

(b)

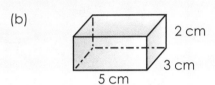

2 cm
3 cm
5 cm

(c)

5 cm
2 cm

(d)

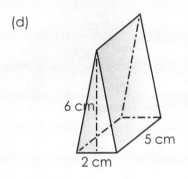

6 cm
5 cm
2 cm

## QUICK TASKS

- Find out what you can about the 'eureka can' and what use it is.

- How would you find the volume of liquid in the bottle without taking out the cork?

  You'll need a ruler.

  Here's a puzzle: How would you find the capacity of the bottle?

  (Capacity is the total volume the container can hold.)

  Challenge others to find out how to do it.

# NUMBER, MEASURE AND MONEY

## OUR EVERYDAY LIVES:

A heating engineer will need to find the volume of rooms and roof spaces if he is to estimate the amount of heating needed for a house.

Here are his instructions:

- For an upstairs room multiply the volume by 148

- For a downstairs room multiply the volume by 185.

  This gives you the amount of heat needed (in units called BTUs).

- Look up the table to get the size of radiator needed.

  Go for the nearest size.

  Downsize if it's a bedroom, upsize if it's a bathroom or hallway.

| Length of radiator (mm) | Heat needed (BTUs) |
|---|---|
| 500 | 3900 |
| 600 | 4300 |
| 700 | 5800 |
| 800 | 6500 |
| 900 | 7400 |
| 1000 | 8000 |
| 1100 | 8500 |
| 1200 | 9000 |

Downsize means 'take the radiator one size down from what the calculation would suggest is needed'.

Work out the length of radiator needed for each of the following rooms.

A downstairs living room

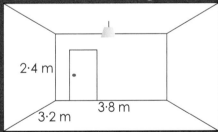

2·4 m
3·8 m
3·2 m

An upstairs bedroom

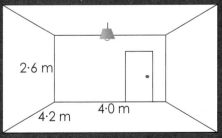

2·6 m
4·0 m
4·2 m

The living room: 2·4 × 3·2 × 3·8 × 185 = 5399 BTU … Table suggests a 700 mm radiator.

The bedroom: 2·6 × 4·2 × 4·0 × 148 = 6465 BTU … Table suggests an 800 mm radiator, but when we downsize we get another 700 mm radiator.

47

# MEASUREMENT

## PYRAMIDS

Pick a point on the top surface of a prism. Join the vertices of the base to this point.

You will define a pyramid related to the prism.

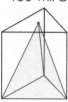 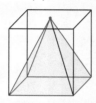   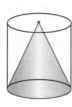

| triangular pyramid | square-based pyramid | pentagonal pyramid | hexagonal pyramid | cone |

The volume of a pyramid is one third of the volume of the related prism.

### Example

The Pyramid of Cheops has a square base of side 230 m.

Its height is 146 m.

Estimate the volume of stone used.

### Response

Volume $= \frac{1}{3} \times$ Area of base $\times$ Height

$= \frac{1}{3} \times 230^2 \times 146$

$= 2574466 \cdot 7 \approx 2570{,}000 \text{ m}^3$

146 m

## THE SPHERE

Archimedes (see Did You Know?) discovered that the sphere was two thirds of the volume of the cylinder into which it just fitted.

He was so pleased with this discovery, they say it was put on his tombstone.

$V = \frac{2}{3}$ area of base $\times$ height

$= \frac{2}{3} \times \pi \times r^2 \times 2r = \frac{4}{3}\pi r^3$

$r$ cm

## COMPOSITE SHAPES

Some solids are made by 'adding' solids together.

### Examples

A house is a cuboid with a triangular prism on top.
A farm silo is a cylinder with a hemisphere on top.
A bell tower is a cuboid with a square-based pyramid on top.

Some solids are made by 'subtracting' one solid from another.

The **frustrum** of a cone is one cone subtracted from another.

The feeding trough is a cuboid with a triangular prism removed.

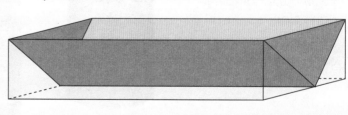

E ACTIVE

## QUICK TESTS

1. Find the volume of each shape.

(a)

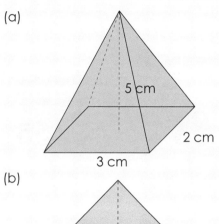

5 cm

2 cm

3 cm

(b)

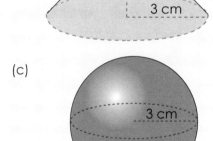

2 cm

3 cm

(c)

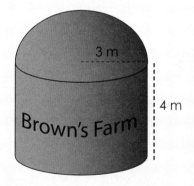

3 cm

2. Calculate the volume of the silo.

3 m

4 m

Brown's Farm

## QUICK TASKS

- Weight is closely related to volume.

  What does a litre of water weigh?

  Weigh a bottle empty and then with a litre of water in it.

  What volume of water weighs a tonne?

  Explore the idea of density.

- Explore the connection between the capacity of a fridge and its cost.

## MAKE THE LINK

- **Physics** – the measurement of volume plays a big part in many areas of physics, including: the Archimedes Principle, the law of flotation, the gas laws, critical mass.

- **Chemistry** – many experiments depend on a strict control of the volumes of quantities mixed. Density of materials (weight of 1 cm$^3$) plays a big part in calculations.

- **History** – the incident known as 'The Black Hole of Calcutta' can be discussed. In 1756, 146 prisoners were held in a room which had a floor space of 25 m$^2$ and a ceiling height of 2 m. 123 of the prisoners died.

- **Geography** – erosion on a river bank depends on the velocity of the water and the volume of the water flow.

- **Home Economics** – volume is a large factor when considering cooking times.

49

## DID YOU KNOW?

Archimedes, an ancient Greek scholar, was instructed by his king, Hiero of Syracuse, to figure out a way of finding the volume of his crown.

Archimedes was pondering the problem when he went for a bath. He noticed the water rising as he got in and realised that the amount of space he occupied was displacing that same volume of water. The story goes that in his excitement, he jumped out of the bath and ran to the palace shouting, 'Eureka!', which means 'I've found it'. In his excitement, he forgot to get dressed first.

He set a beaker filled with water inside a basin, and placed the crown in it. The water spilling over the edge was caught in the basin and measured. The volume of water thus measured was the same as the volume of the crown.

This experimental way of finding the volume of awkward shapes is still used today, but for some basic shapes we have figured out formulae.

# PATTERNS AND RELATIONSHIPS

## FAMOUS PATTERNS

The natural numbers

The even numbers

The odd numbers

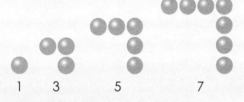

The square numbers

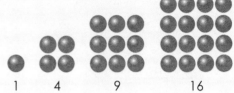

The triangular numbers

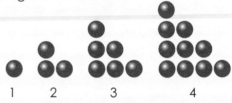

## THE GENERAL TERM

In order to study sequences better, mathematicians have come up with a special set of symbols.

Each sequence has a 1st term, a 2nd term, a 3rd term, and so on.

In general we talk about the $n^{th}$ term.

We use a letter to stand for a term and add a subscript to say which term it is.

We might use $u$ and so $u_1$ is the 1st term, $u_2$ is the second term, $u_3$ is the 3rd term, and we use $u_n$ to stand for the $n^{th}$ term.

What is really useful is when a formula can be found for the general term.

- We might represent the first square number by $s_1$.
  So $s_1 = 1, s_2 = 4, s_3 = 9, s_4 = 16, s_5 = 25$ ... and $s_n = n^2$
- The multiples of 6: $u_1 = 6, u_2 = 12, u_3 = 18,$ ... and $u_n = 6n$
- A simple pattern: $u_1 = 2, u_2 = 3, u_3 = 4,$ ... and $u_n = n + 1$
- A relative of the multiples of 6: $u_1 = 5, u_2 = 11, u_3 = 17, u_4 = 23,$ ... and $u_n = 6n - 1$
  Having a formula for its $n^{th}$ term will allow us to build up a sequence.

### EXAMPLE 1

Give the first three terms of the sequence which has an nth term, $u_n = 3n + 2$

**Response**

$u_1 = 3.1 + 2 = 5$
$u_2 = 3.2 + 2 = 8$
$u_3 = 3.3 + 2 = 11$

### EXAMPLE 2

Janet was given a bank account with £150 in it. She was allowed to take out £8 each week. The amount in the account at the start of each week formed a pattern with $n^{th}$ term $u_n = 150 - 8u$.

(a) Give the first 3 terms of the sequence.
(b) Work out the 10th term in the sequence.

**Response**

(a) $u_1 = 150 - 8.1 = 150 - 8 = 142$
$u_2 = 150 - 8.2 = 150 - 16 = 134$
$u_3 = 150 - 8.3 = 150 - 24 = 126$
(b) $u_{10} = 150 - 8.10 = 150 - 80 = 70$

## BE ACTIVE

## QUICK TESTS

1. Find the first 5 terms of each sequence:

   (a) $u_n = 4n + 3$

   (b) $u_n = 5n - 3$

   (c) $u_n = 77 - 3n$

   (d) $u_n = n^2 + 1$

   (e) $u_n = 2(n - 1)(n - 2)(n - 3) + n$

2. If there were sets of dominoes that only went up to double-blank there would only be one domino in the set. If they went to double-1 there would be three. If they went to double-2 there would be six. The picture shows the double-2 set.

   (a) What number pattern is building up?

   (b) How many dominoes are there in a set that goes up to double-6?

   (c) You can buy sets that go up to double-9. How many are in that set?

## QUICK TASKS

- I googled 'Fibonacci numbers' and got 455 000 hits. Explore Fibonacci numbers on the internet and make a report.

- Pascal was a famous French mathematician. He drew a pattern of numbers to the attention of the world at large. It is called Pascal's triangle.

  It starts with a 1

  Underneath put 1 1

  Each new row starts and ends with a 1

```
            1
          1   1
        1   2   1
      1   3   3   1
    1   4   6   4   1
  1   5  10  10   5   1
```

  In between, each entry is the sum of the two entries above it. Continue this triangle for seven rows.

  Scrutinise it for patterns, old ones and new ones.

  Write a report.

# NUMBER, MEASURE AND MONEY

## MAKE THE LINK

- **Physics** – the study of half-life will generate sequences.

- **Biology** – spiral patterns on seed heads, fir-cones and leaves all seem to produce Fibonacci numbers.

- **Chemistry** – the families of organic chemical compounds, a count of the carbon atoms and hydrogen atoms form sequences.

## DID YOU KNOW?

The ancient Greeks explored numbers by considering the patterns they could make with pebbles. It is interesting to note that the Romans used pebbles to help them count and their word for a pebble is 'calculus' ... from which we get our word 'calculate'.

**51**

## OUR EVERYDAY LIVES:

We can use the 'pebbles' idea to look for relationships among the patterns. You make the triangular numbers by adding together the natural numbers.

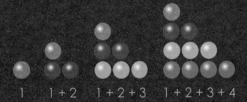

1     1 + 2     1 + 2 + 3     1 + 2 + 3 + 4

You build up the square numbers by adding together the odd numbers.

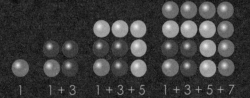

1     1 + 3     1 + 3 + 5     1 + 3 + 5 + 7

You make square numbers by adding two neighbouring triangular numbers.

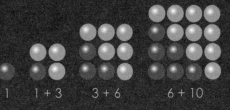

1     1 + 3     3 + 6     6 + 10

# PATTERNS AND RELATIONSHIPS

## FINDING A FORMULA FOR $u_n$

In many cases we can work out what the formula for the $n^{th}$ term should be. Sometimes the sequence is a multiplication table 'in disguise'.

### Example 1

We know the 3-times table goes up in threes: 3, 6, 9, 12, ... with $u_n = 3n$

Write down the $n^{th}$ term of the sequence

(a) 4, 7, 10, 13, ...

(b) 2, 5, 8, 11, ...

(c) 1, 4, 7, 10, ...

(d) 10, 13, 16, 19, ...

### Response

In each case the terms go up in threes, like the 3-times table. By looking at the first term in each case we can see what has been added to or subtracted from 3 ...

(a) 4 is 3 + 1 ... the $n^{th}$ term is $3n + 1$

(b) 2 is 3 − 1 ... the $n^{th}$ term is $3n − 1$

(c) 1 is 3 − 2 ... the $n^{th}$ term is $3n − 2$

(d) 10 is 3 + 7 ... the $n^{th}$ term is $3n + 7$

If we assume that the 'obvious' pattern continues then this method can be used to find the $n^{th}$ terms of similar patterns.

**TOP TIP**

If you are not told that a pattern continues then you have to be careful.

There are lots of patterns which start with 1, 2, 3, ..

There is the 'obvious' one: $u_n = n$ ... which gives 1, 2, 3, 4, 5, ...

But what about the rule: $u_n = ((n − 6)n + 12)n − 6$ ?

This formula can be better imagined as the function machine

this gives 1, 2, 3, 10, 29, ...

However, for the rest of the examples we will assume that the 'obvious' pattern does continue.

The $n^{th}$ term of some other patterns can be worked out by considering the 'pebble' patterns.

Take the triangular numbers

Double each one and rearrange to form rectangles

Now you can see that the 'double triangular number' pattern is $1 × 2$, $2 × 3$, $3 × 4$, $4 × 5$, ...

It's clear to see that the nth term of this pattern is $n × (n + 1)$, or just $n(n + 1)$.

Halving this will get us back to the triangular numbers: $t_n = \frac{1}{2}n(n + 1)$.

Armed with this you could work out any of the triangular numbers. What is $t_{24}$?

## BE ACTIVE

## QUICK TESTS

1. Find a formula for the $n^{th}$ term of each sequence:

   (a) 6, 8, 10, 12, ...

   (b) 5, 15, 25, 35, ...

   (c) 20, 17, 14, 11, ...

   (d) 3, 6, 11, 18, ... (Hint: Think of the squares.)

## QUICK TASKS

- You can use Excel to explore the patterns created by different formulae.

  In A1 type: 1

  In A2 type: = A1 + 1 and fill this down column A. You have now created the ns

  i.e. 1st, 2nd, 3rd, 4th, etc

  In B1 enter the $n$th term e.g. : = 3*A1 + 5 ( ... to explore $u_n = 3n + 5$)

  Try this:

  In A1 type: 1

  In A2 type 1:

  In A3 type: = A1 + A2 and fill down... the Fibonacci sequence.

- Take a newspaper apart and look at the numbering of facing pages.

  For example, when I took today's newspaper apart, one sheet contained pages 1, 2, 29 and 30. Pages 2 and 29 were facing each other. Explore this idea and look for patterns and connections.

- Look at the calendar ... pick a month, say April:

| April 2009 | | | | | | |
|---|---|---|---|---|---|---|
| Sun | Mon | Tues | Wed | Thurs | Fri | Sat |
|  |  |  | 1 | 2 | 3 | 4 |
| 5 | 6 | 7 | 8 | 9 | 10 | 11 |
| 12 | 13 | 14 | 15 | 16 | 17 | 18 |
| 19 | 20 | 21 | 22 | 23 | 24 | 25 |
| 26 | 27 | 28 | 29 | 30 |  |  |

  Now explore the formula that produces the sequence of Wednesdays.

  Look for other sequences, e.g. the 1st Sunday with the 2nd Monday and the 3rd Tuesday, etc.

# NUMBER, MEASURE AND MONEY

## MAKE THE LINK

- **Geography** – population growth can be modelled using sequences. Quite often a formula which turns one term into the next rather than having an nth -term formula is used.

- **Mathematics** – for centuries mathematicians have hunted for a pattern in the primes. Primes have been used to create codes, as there seems to be no pattern in them.

- **IT** – patterns are a major feature of the use of Excel spreadsheets.

## OUR EVERYDAY LIVES:

53

(a) On the left-hand side of a terrace, the houses are numbered 158, 156, 154, 152 and so on. Joe has told us that he lives in the 50th house on the left. How is it numbered?

(b) Down the right hand side the houses are numbered 157, 155, 153, 151 and so on. The postman has a letter for No. 55. How far down the road is that if each house has a front of length of 8 metres?

**Response**

(a) The sequence starts at 158 and goes down in twos. The $n^{th}$ term is therefore $u_n = 160 - 2n$

   For $n = 50$ we get $u_{50} = 160 - 2.50 = 60$
   Joe's house is numbered '60'.

(b) The sequence starts at 157 and goes down in twos. The $n^{th}$ term is therefore $u_n = 159 - 2n$

   With a bit of trial and error we can see that the 50th term is $159 - 100 = 59$; the 51st is 57, and the 52nd is 55.

   The distance he needs to walk = 8 × 52 = 416 metres.

# EXPRESSIONS AND EQUATIONS

## NOTATION

### MULTIPLICATION

You already know that in mathematics we often use letters to stand for numbers.

Since they stand for numbers, they behave like numbers.

**Let's establish the rules.**

We know $6 + 6 + 6 + 6$ is four sixes and can be written $4 \times 6$ or $4.6$

We know $4 + 4 + 4 + 4 + 4 + 4$ is six fours and can be written $6 \times 4$ or $6.4$

Suppose $x$ stands for some number.

Then $x + x + x + x$ is four $x$s and can be written $4 \times x$ or $4.x$ and is written $4x$.

We know $4 + 4 + ... + 4 + 4$ (for $x$ terms) is $x$ fours and can be written $x \times 4$ or $x.4$

- $4x = 4 \times x$

If y is another number, $y + y + ... + y + y$ (for $x$ terms) is $x$ $y$s and can be written $x \times y$ or $x.y$ usually written $xy$.

We know that six fours = four sixes = 24

In a similar way $4x = x.4$ and $xy = yx$

- $yx = yx$

When we multiply a number by itself we get results like:

$x \times x = xx$ or even $x \times x \times x = xxx$
or $x \times x \times x \times x = xxxx$

We have a shorthand to cope with this:

$xx = x^2$, $xxx = x^3$, $xxxx = x^4$, and so on.

However, please remember that $x^2$ does not equal $2x$

- $xx = x^2$

In the multiplication $3 \times 5 \times 7 \times 2$ we can rearrange the factors to suit ourselves, changing the order in which we do the calculations:

$3 \times 5 \times 7 \times 2$
$$= 2 \times 5 \times 3 \times 7$$
$$= 10 \times 21$$
$$= 210$$

This also happens when letters are involved.

**Example**
Multiply $3x$ by $4xy$

**Response**
$3x \times 4xy = 3 \times x \times 4 \times x \times y$
$$= 3 \times 4 \times x \times x \times y$$
$$= 12x^2y$$

### ADDITION AND SUBTRACTION

The order in which you add doesn't matter ...
$3 + 5 = 5 + 3$

- $x + y = y + x$

We know 3 fives and 4 fives makes 7 fives ...
$3.5 + 4.5 = 7.5$

We can see this by going back to basics:

$(5 + 5 + 5) + (5 + 5 + 5 + 5)$

$= 5 + 5 + 5 + 5 + 5 + 5 + 5$

$3x + 4x$
$= (3 + 4)x$
$= 7x$

In the same way $3x + 4x = 7x$

$3x$ and $4x$ are known as like terms.

- **like terms can be combined in addition and subtraction**

This can be taken one step further …

- $yx + zx = (y + z)x$

Which can be rearranged to give us a handy rule:

- $x(y + z) = xy + xz$

$yx + zx$
$= (y + z)x$

**Example**
Find another expression for $3(x + 2)$.

**Response**
$3(x + 2) = x + 2 + x + 2 + x + 2 = 3x + 3.2 = 3x + 6$

Of course, we usually skip all the 'in-between' steps:

$3(x + 2) = 3x + 6$

We don't get the same convenient simplification if we have 3 fives and 4 sixes.

Similarly, if $x$ and $y$ stand for two numbers, $3x + 4y$ doesn't simplify further.

$3x$ and $4y$ are known as unlike terms.

- **unlike terms cannot be combined in addition and subtraction**

**DIVISION**
The division $10 \div 2 = 5$ can be written as $\frac{10}{2} = 5$.

This is the usual way of writing it when working with letters.

**Example**
$\frac{x}{2} = x \div 2$; $\frac{10}{x} = 10 \div x$; $\frac{x}{y} = x \div y$; $\frac{x+2}{3} = (x + 2) \div 3$

Just as fractions can be simplified by 'cancelling' common factors in the numerator and denominator, we can do it when working with letters.

You can divide a sum of terms by dividing each term separately before you add.

For example,

$\frac{6+9}{3} = \frac{6}{3} + \frac{9}{3} = 2 + 3 = 5$

… and we knew

$\frac{6+9}{3} = \frac{15}{3} = 5$

We can do the same with letters:

$\frac{6x+9}{3} = \frac{6x}{3} + \frac{9}{3} = 2x + 3$

**Example**
Simplify $\frac{60}{45}$

**Response**
$\frac{60}{45} = \frac{2.2.3.5}{3.3.5} = \frac{2.2}{3} = \frac{4}{3}$

… in actual practice we need not actually show all the factors.

$$\frac{A^2 + B^2}{Y^2 + X}$$

55

**BE ACTIVE**

## QUICK TESTS

Simplify:

1.  (a) $2a + 3a$
    (b) $3a + 5b + 2a - 2b$
    (c) $2x + 5 + 3x + 2$
    (d) $3x \times 5x$
    (e) $4xy \times 6x$
    (f) $\frac{10\,xy^2}{3x^2y}$
    (g) $4(x + 3)$

## QUICK TASKS

*   You can make Excel spreadsheets work with algebraic expressions.

    (1) Select A1

    (2) You will see A1 appear in a box in the menu bar

    ... this is called the 'Name' box.

    (3) Click in the Name box and change A1 to '$x$'.

    (4) In A1 put a number, say, 5

    (5) In B1 type: $= 2 + x$   ... 7 will appear.

    Try a variety of expressions. See them at work.

    You will need to use * for multiplication, / for division and ^ to get squares and cubes (e.g. $x$^2 means $x^2$).

    Change the number in A1 and watch the value of the expressions change.

    $x$ and the expressions are called variables ... since their values are changeable.

    The values in the boxes containing expressions are often called dependent variables, depending as they do on the value of $x$.

    (6) In A2 add a second variable called $y$. Build up expressions using $x$ and $y$.

    Watch how their value changes as $x$ and $y$ change.

## MAKE THE LINK

*   **Science** – algebraic expressions are a mainstay of Physics, Chemistry and Biology.

*   **Geography** – economic models and weather models make use of algebra.

*   **Mathematics** – these expressions are essential for the development of algebra, solving equations and exploring patterns.

*   **IT** – knowledge of algebraic expressions are essential for the use of Excel spreadsheets.

## DID YOU KNOW?

There is a famous trick:

'Think of a number. Double it. Add 10. Halve it. Take away the number you first thought of. Your answer is 5.'

How do you know you'll be right no matter what number the other person thinks of?

**Response**
Use algebra to form an expression from the instructions:

| | |
|---|---|
| 'Think of a number: | $x$ |
| Double it | $= 2x$ |
| Add 10 | $= 2x + 10$ |
| Halve it | $= x + 5$ |
| Take away the number you first thought of | $= x + 5 - x$ |
| Your answer is 5.' | $= 5$ |

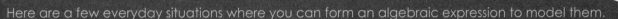

## OUR EVERYDAY LIVES:

Here are a few everyday situations where you can form an algebraic expression to model them.

(a) Karen bought five litres of milk. She paid with a single note and got 25p change.

Let $x$ pence be the cost of a litre of milk. Write an expression for the note.

(b) Deirdre filled six glasses from her bottle of tomato juice, leaving 20 ml in the bottle.

Let $y$ ml be the contents of a single glass. Give an expression for the full bottle.

(c) Katrona had to write an essay of 2000 words. She wanted to write the same number of words a day. Write an expression for the number of words she should write if the essay had to be done in $z$ days.

(d) Dorothy had been shopping. Her bag contained five tins of juice, two bottles of milk and a kilogram bag of sugar. Write an expression for the weight of her bag assuming a tin of juice weighs $n$ g and a bottle of milk weighs $m$ g.

**Response**

(a) $5x + 25$ pence

(b) $6y + 20$ ml

(c) $\frac{2000}{z}$ words per day

(d) $5n + 2m + 1000$ grams

# EXPRESSIONS AND EQUATIONS

## EQUATIONS

Karen bought five litres of milk. She paid with a £5 note and got 25p change. What is the cost of a litre of milk?

An expression for the note is $(5x + 25)$ pence where $x$ is the cost in pence of one litre of milk.

Now, the note is a £5 note ... 500 pence.

So $5x + 25 = 500$

Any expression like this is called an equation. It's an equation because the left-hand side equals the right-hand side.

We can replace $x$ with a number

e.g. let $x = 4$ this would lead to 5.4 + 25 = 500 or 45 = 500 which is plainly false.

let $x = 10$ this would lead to 5.10 + 25 = 500 or 75 = 500 which is also false.

let $x = 95$ this would lead to 5.95 + 25 = 500 or 500 = 500 which is true.

The value of $x$ which makes the equation true is called its solution. We don't need to use trial and error to find the solution.

**TOP TIP**
Remember the rule, 'Do the same thing to both sides'.

### EXAMPLE

Imagine the equation is a set of scales. At the moment it is balanced. As long as you do the same thing to both sides, it will stay balanced. Follow this:

$5x + 25 = 500$

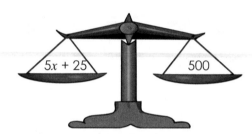

Take 25 from both sides

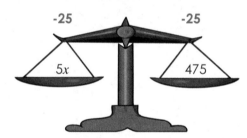

$\Rightarrow 5x = 475$

Divide both sides by 5

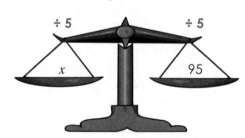

$\Rightarrow x = 95$

Your aim is to end up with the unknown on one pan of the scales and a number on the other. You can choose any steps you like as long as you stick to the rule, 'Do the same thing to both sides'.

Some sets of steps get you there quicker and easier than others.

58

### ...E ACTIVE

## ...UICK TESTS

1. Solve the following equations

   (a) $6x + 5 = 29$

   (b) $8c - 2 = 22$

   (c) $100 - 5x = 60$

   (d) $x - 30 = \frac{x}{4}$

   (e) $7x + 1 = 10x - 17$

2. On a particular bus route I wanted to go for 8 stages.

   I paid with a note and got £2·60 change.

   (a) Form an expression for the value of the note using £$x$ to stand for the fare for one stage.

   (b) If the note were £5, form an equation and solve it to find the cost of one fare stage.

## ...UICK TASKS

- You can make a spreadsheet hunt for a solution to an equation if the solution is a whole number.

  In A1 type: 1; in A2 type: = A1 + 1; fill down to row 10

  Suppose you wish to solve $3x + 4 = 19$ then in B1 type: = 3*A1 + 4 = 19

  (Note the extra = sign at the start of the equation and that A1 is being used for $x$.)

  Fill down to row 10.

  The word 'FALSE' will appear all the way down except at the solution, 5, where the entry reads 'TRUE'.

  If no cell reads TRUE then change A1 to 11, then 21, etc.

  Explore the possibilities.

## MAKE THE LINK

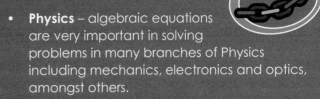

- **Physics** – algebraic equations are very important in solving problems in many branches of Physics including mechanics, electronics and optics, amongst others.

- **Chemistry** – the notion behind balanced equations is used when working with chemical equations.

- **Mathematics** – equations are the basis of problem-solving as well as the construction of formulae (which are really just equations).

## DID YOU KNOW?

The French Mathematician François Viète used $x$ and $y$ in equations for the first time in 1591.

## OUR EVERYDAY LIVES:

Many practical problems can be solved if you can first form an equation.

Sometimes assumptions have to be made to allow the equation to be formed.

### For example

A small car ferry connecting the Western Isles has an International Load Line painted on its side to make sure that it never gets overloaded.

A record tells us that the last time the ferry was fully laden there were 16 cars and 2·4 tonnes of cargo. On a previous occasion, a full load was 14 cars and 4·8 tonnes of cargo.

How much cargo could be carried on board if there were 13 cars?

(Hint: let $x$ be the weight of 1 car.)

## MAKE THE LINK

# FORMULAE

## FORMULAE

You have already looked at formulae when studying area and volume.

For each of the basic shapes there is a method for finding the area and for each of the basic solids a method for finding the volume.

These are most usefully expressed as a formula.

They can also be expressed in words or in symbols

They both have their place; words tend to be easier to understand to those who haven't learned to read symbols. Symbols give a neater picture often easier to remember.

Easy formulae in everyday life are those for converting one unit into another.

### EXAMPLE

(i)  $c = 100m$  ... converts $m$ metres into $c$ centimetres.

(ii)  $d = 1\cdot4p$  ... converts £$p$ to \$$d$ (true in 2009)

(iii)  $m = \frac{8k}{5}$  ... converts $k$ kilometres to $m$ miles

(iv)  $A = \pi r^2$  ... works out the area, $A$ units$^2$, of a circle of radius $r$ units ($\pi$ is approximately $3\cdot14$ ... usually a button on the calculator.)

Formulae will often connect more than two variables.

### Example 1

If we want to estimate what length of carpet ($L$ m) is needed for a staircase we need to know how many steps there are ($s$), the height of a riser ($r$ m) and the length of a tread ($t$ m).

The formula is $L = sr + (s - 1)t$

Not counting either 'landing':

(a) Calculate the length of carpet needed for 6 steps whose risers are 0·16 m and whose treads are 0·25 m.

(b) A staircase had 14 steps. Its risers were of length 0·18 m. It took 6·42 m of carpet to cover it. How big were the treads?

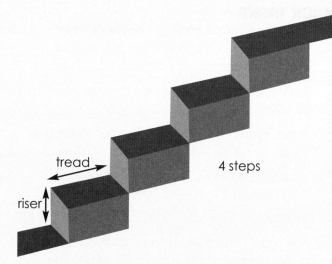

tread    4 steps

riser

### Response

(a) $L = sr + (s - 1)t$
Substituting we get
$L = 6 \times 0\cdot16 + (6 - 1) \times 0\cdot25 = 2\cdot21$ m
We need 2·21 m of carpet.

(b) $L = sr + (s - 1)t$
Substituting we get $6\cdot42 = 14 \times 0\cdot18 + 13t$
Tidying up we get an equation to solve:

$6\cdot42 = 2\cdot52 + 13t$  ... subtract 2·52 from both sides

$\Rightarrow 13t = 3\cdot9$  ... divide by 13

$\Rightarrow t = 0\cdot3$

The treads will be 0·30 m long.

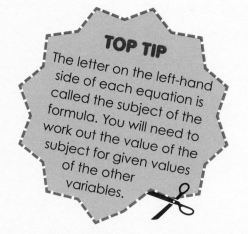

**TOP TIP**

The letter on the left-hand side of each equation is called the subject of the formula. You will need to work out the value of the subject for given values of the other variables.

60

# ND MONEY * NUMBER,

## E ACTIVE

### QUICK TESTS

1. Evaluate the subject of each formula.

   (a) $T = 4e + 5$ when $e = 7$

   (b) $G = 100 - 12k$ when $k = 5$

   (c) $F = \frac{g_1 g_2}{d}$ when $g_1 = 6$, $g_2 = 15$, and $d = 10$

2. A wind farm calculates the power that a wind turbine generates, $W$ watts, by using the formula: $W = 2r^2 v^3$ where $r$ metres is the length of a blade and $v$ metres per second is the wind velocity.

   (a) What power can be generated by a turbine with a 10 m blade in a wind blowing at 12 m/s?

   (b) How much power is generated from a farm containing 10 turbines each of which has blades of length 8 m when the wind is 8 m/s?

### QUICK TASKS

- You don't know how to solve the equation $x^2 - x - 2 = 0$ but if you guess the answer is $g$ then the formula $G = \frac{2}{g} + 1$ will produce a better guess.

  Make a guess, say 4 ... type 4 = into your calculator.

  Type: 2 ÷ ANS + 1 = and a better guess will be produced. Each time you type =, a better guess will appear. Explore what happens when you press = lots of times.

  A similar formula for $x^2 - 3x - 10 = 0$ is $G = \frac{10}{g} + 3$

  Check it out.

  Can you devise a formula for $x^2 - 4x - 21 = 0$ ?

- Comparing taxi firms:
  *Personal Touch Taxis* has a formula for charging customers $F = 1 \cdot 56m + 2$ where $£F$ is the fare for a journey of $m$ miles. *Swift Luxury Limos'* formula is different; $F = 1 \cdot 65m + 1$

  For a 1-mile journey, *Swift Luxury Limos* charges £2·65 and *Personal Touch Taxis* charges £3·56. *Swift Luxury Limos* is better.

  For a 20-mile journey, *Swift Luxury Limos* charges £34·00 and *Personal Touch Taxis* charges £33·20. *Personal Touch* is better.

  Explore the situation.

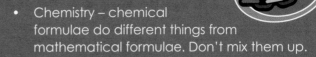
## MAKE THE LINK

- Chemistry – chemical formulae do different things from mathematical formulae. Don't mix them up.

- Geography – use formulae in spreadsheets to work out averages when exploring weather, river flow, population densities.

## DID YOU KNOW?

The two most common ways to measure temperature are the Fahrenheit scale and the Celsius scale. Although Celsius is the most common, many recipe books still use the Fahrenheit scale.

This formula will turn Fahrenheit temperatures into Celsius.

$C = \frac{F - 32}{1 \cdot 8}$

## OUR EVERYDAY LIVES:

In real-life situations formulae are often used as a guide rather than as a hard accurate fact. The results obtained from such formulae should be used with caution.

**Naismith's Formula**
When you go hill-walking you should always let someone know your planned route and your estimated time of return.
William Naismith in 1892 devised a formula that many people use.
It works out the time of the walk, $T$ hours, given the length of the walk, $L$ km, your average walking speed, $s$ km/h, the climbs (all the uphill bits), $c$ m and the descents (all the downhill bits), $d$ m.
$T = \frac{L}{s} + 0 \cdot 0017c + 0 \cdot 0008d$
Peter sets out on a 15 km hike. Looking at the map he sees that overall he will be gaining height for 800 m and losing the height for 700 m. Peter knows he tends to walk at 3·5 km per hour. Use the formula to estimate the time his trek will take.

# PROPERTIES OF 2D SHAPES AND 3D OBJECTS

### DRAWING TRIANGLES 1

A yacht is anchored in the bay. How might we find its distance from the shore?

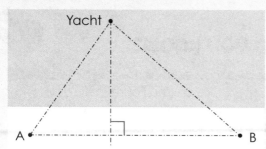

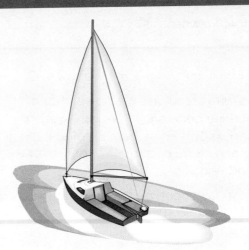

On the shore mark two points A and B, 100 metres apart. From A take a siting of the yacht, Y, and, using a protractor, measure the angle YAB. At B measure the angle YBA. Let's say for this example that these are ∠YAB = 54° and ∠YBA = 40°

You can now recreate the triangle ABY and measure the distance from the line AB to Y.

However, drawing a triangle that size is impractical.

But what if you used this ruler?

Here 100 metres have been 'shrunk'. 1 millimetre is being used as 1 metre.

Draw the line AB, '100 metres' long.

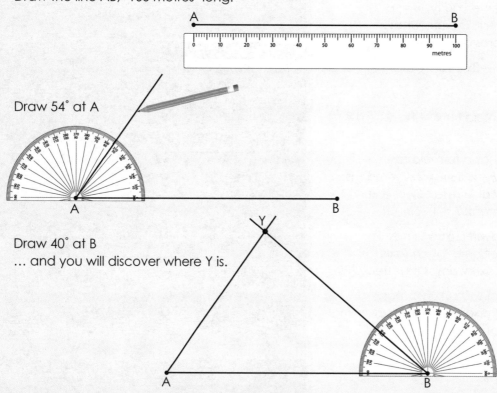

Draw 54° at A

Draw 40° at B
... and you will discover where Y is.

Now use your special ruler to measure the distance you want.

The yacht is 52 metres from the shore.

Being able to draw triangles accurately is very useful and will allow you to solve many problems and find sizes that would otherwise be inaccessible.

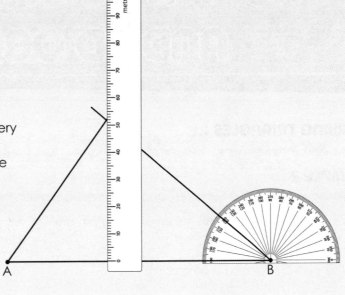

The steps to take depend on the information you have.

## EXAMPLE 1

Suppose you know the lengths of the three sides.

Draw a triangle with sides 6 cm, 8 cm and 9 cm.

You'll need a ruler and a set of compasses.

Step 1: Draw a line, AB of length 9 cm (the longest length)

Step 2: Draw an arc centre A and radius 8 cm

Step 3: Draw an arc centre B and radius 6 cm.

Step 4: Where the arcs cross mark C.

Step 5: Draw ABC, the triangle with sides, 6 cm, 8 cm and 9 cm.

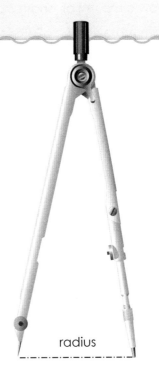

radius

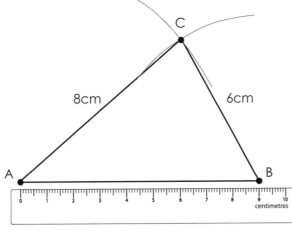

# PROPERTIES OF 2D SHAPES AND 3D OBJECTS

## DRAWING TRIANGLES 2

### EXAMPLE 2

Suppose you're given two sides and the angle between them.

Draw triangle, ABC with AB = 6 cm, AC = 8 cm and ∠CAB = 35°.

You'll need a ruler and a protractor.

Step 1: Draw a line, AB of length 6 cm.

Step 2: From A draw a line at 35° to AB.

Step 3: Mark C, 8 cm along this line.

Step 4: Draw ABC, the triangle with, AB = 6 cm,
AC = 8 cm and ∠CAB = 35°.

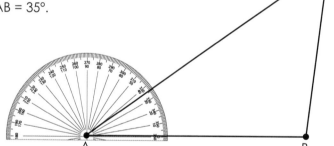

### EXAMPLE 3

What if the angle given is not between the two known sides?

Draw triangle PQR where PQ is 8 cm, QR is 9 cm and ∠QPR = 110°.

Step 1: Draw a line, PQ of length 8 cm.

Step 2: From P draw a line at 110° to PQ.

Step 3: Draw an arc centre Q and radius 9 cm to cross this line at R.

Step 4: Draw PQR, the wanted triangle.

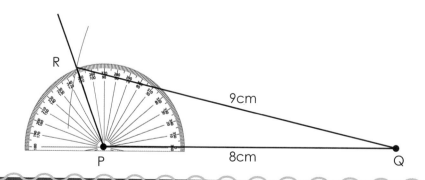

## DID YOU KNOW?

Once Galileo started studying Venus through a telescope, he discovered that it went through phases just like the Moon.

When it looked like a half-Venus, the Earth, Venus and the Sun must have been in these relative positions with ∠SVE = 90°. Now ∠SEV can be measured and has been found to be 46°. We can calculate ∠SEV = 44°.

For the sake of convenience, let's say the distance between the Earth and the Sun is 10 units. Work out the distance between Venus and the Sun.

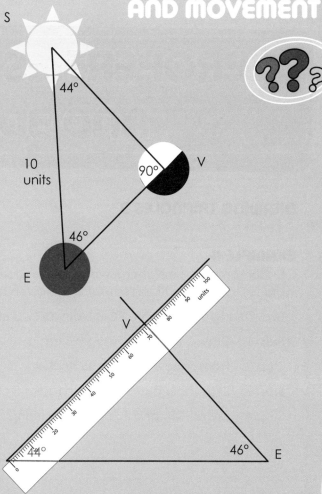

Using a centimetre to be a unit we can draw the triangle accurately and measure the distance.

The distance between Venus and the Sun is 7·2 units.

**All the distances in the Solar system are measured using the Earth/Sun distance as the unit.**

## OUR EVERYDAY LIVES:

Many real problems can be solved by carefully choosing units and drawing appropriate triangles. For example, driving from Glasgow to Edinburgh, you travel the M8 in, roughly speaking, a straight line of length 82 km. Stirling is 43 km from Glasgow and 58 km from Edinburgh.

How close do you get to Stirling on your journey, and how far from Glasgow are you when you get to this point?

Using this ruler, where 1 cm is marked as 10 km we can draw a suitable triangle with Glasgow, Stirling and Edinburgh at its vertices.

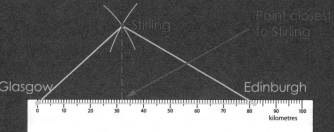

We can pick out the point closest to Stirling.

Measuring gives the information that this point is 32 km from Glasgow.

We get to within 29 km of Stirling.

# PROPERTIES OF 2D SHAPES AND 3D OBJECTS

### DRAWING TRIANGLES 3

#### EXAMPLE 4

Under some circumstances, when following step 3, we find the arc crosses the line at two different places, giving two triangles that fit the given description.

Draw triangle PQR where PQ is 8 cm, QR is 5 cm and $\angle QPR = 35°$.

Step 1:  Draw a line, PQ of length 8 cm

Step 2:  From P draw a line at 35° to PQ

Step 3:  Draw an arc centre Q and radius 5 cm to cross this line at $R_1$ and $R_2$

Step 4:  Draw $PQR_1$ and $PQR_2$ the two triangles that fit the given description.

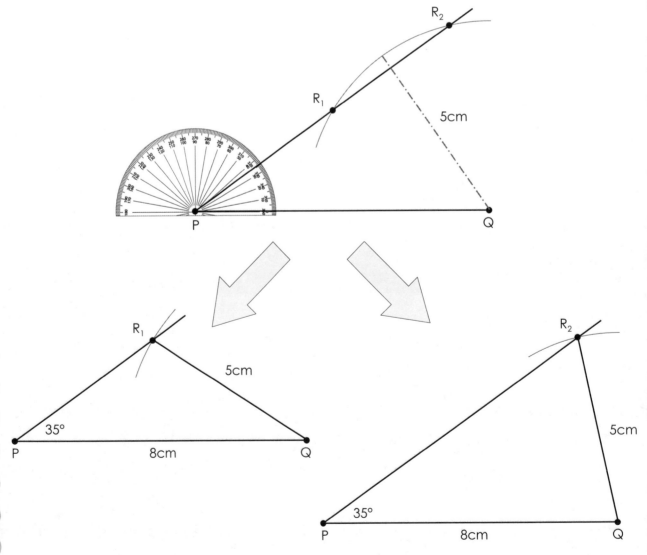

This is called the ambiguous case ... there being two answers for the one set of data.

## BE ACTIVE

### QUICK TESTS

1. Draw the triangle ABC where AB = 8 cm, BC = 7 cm and CA = 6 cm
   Measure the shortest distance between C and AB.

2. Draw the triangle PQR where PQ = 7 cm, PR = 8 cm and ∠QPR = 45°
   Measure the sizes of ∠PQR and ∠QRP.

3. Draw the triangle FGH with FG = 9 cm, ∠HFG = 40° and ∠HGF = 50°
   Measure the perimeter of the triangle.

4. Draw two triangles to fit the description AB = 8 cm, BC = 6 cm and ∠CAB = 40°. Give the size of ∠ABC for each.

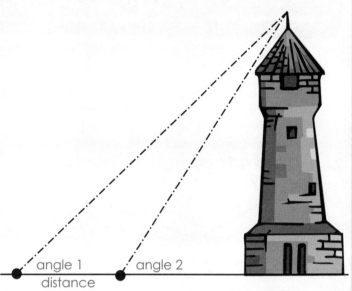

### QUICK TASKS

- Find the height of the school or a nearby spire. Take just enough measurements to allow you to draw a triangle.

- Research how the length of the metre was invented. The map shows how the scientists worked out the distance between Paris and Dunkirk using triangles.

- Study the ambiguous case and decide the conditions that cause it, e.g. use lengths AB = 8 cm and BC = 6 cm and find out the angle ∠BAC that first gives two answers.

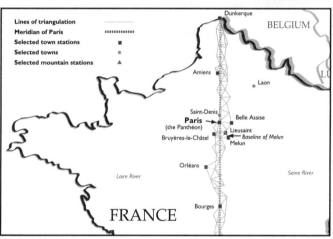

67

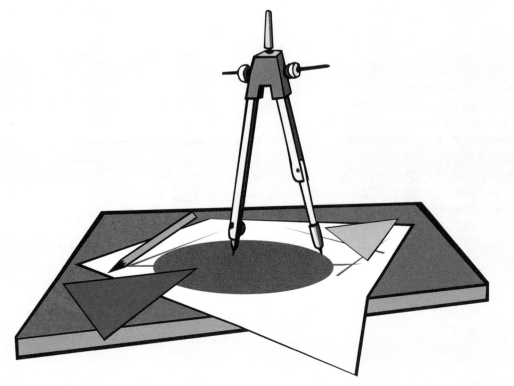

# PROPERTIES OF 2D SHAPES AND 3D OBJECTS

## ANGLES

In many situations angles are related and knowing the size of one will allow you to work out others without the need to measure. To help you, many of these relationships have been given names.

- **Angles round a point add up to 360°**
  Knowing this allows you to work out that
  $x = 110$

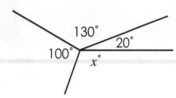

- **Supplementary angles add up to 180°**
  Supplements form a straight line.
  60° and $y°$ are supplements.
  So $y = 120$.

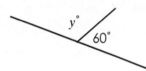

- **Complementary angles add up to 90°**
  Complements form a right angle.
  50° and $z°$ are complements.
  So $z = 40$.

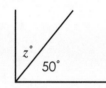

- **Vertically opposite angles are equal**
  When two straight lines intersect they form two pairs of vertically opposite angles.
  $a°$ is the supplement of 20°. So $a = 160$.
  $b°$ is the supplement of $a°$. So $b = 20$.
  $c°$ is the supplement of $b°$. So $c = 120$.
  Vertically opposite angles are equal.

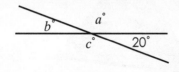

- **Angles associated with parallel lines**
  When a single line cuts two parallel lines the pattern of angles round one intersection is identical to the pattern round the other.

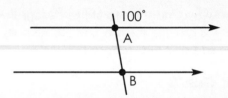

Knowing only the angle marked 100° and using supplements and vertically opposite angles we can deduce the angles round A.

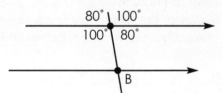

The pattern round B is the same as the pattern round A. … and so the finished diagram looks like this.

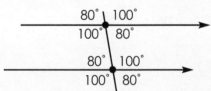

By looking only at parts of this diagram we can find other useful relationships.

- **Alternate angles are equal**

Look for the zig-zag (or Z-angles)

- **Corresponding angles are equal**

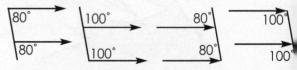

Look for the F-angles

68

- **Co-interior angles are supplementary**

Look for the C-angles

We can now explore the properties of shapes.

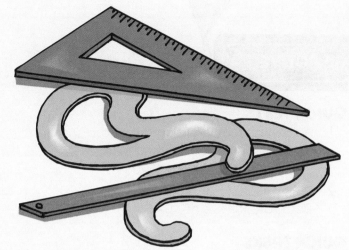

## EXAMPLE 1

What is the sum of the angles in a triangle?

**Response**

Draw a line TCP parallel to AB

We can deduce $\angle TCA = a°$ (alternate angles)

$\angle PCB = b°$ (alternate angles)

$\angle TCP = \angle TCA + \angle PCB + \angle ACB$

$= a° + b° + c°$

But $\angle TCP$ is a straight angle

So $a° + b° + c° = 180°$

So the angles of a triangle add up to 180°.

## EXAMPLE 2

Find all the angles in the rectangle.

**Response**

$\angle TPQ = 55°$ (complement of $\angle RPS$)

$\angle TQP = 55°$ (by symmetry of rectangle)

$\angle PTQ = 70°$ (third angle of triangle QPT)

$\angle QTR = 110°$ (supplement of $\angle PTQ$)

$\angle RTS = 70°$ (vertically opposite $\angle PTQ$)

$\angle PTS = 110°$ (vertically opposite $\angle QTR$)

$\angle QRT = 35°$ (alternate to $\angle RPS$)

$\angle TQR = 35°$ (complement of $\angle PQT$)

$\angle QSP = 35°$ (alternate to $\angle RQS$)

$\angle PRS = \angle QSR = 55°$ (by symmetry of rectangle)

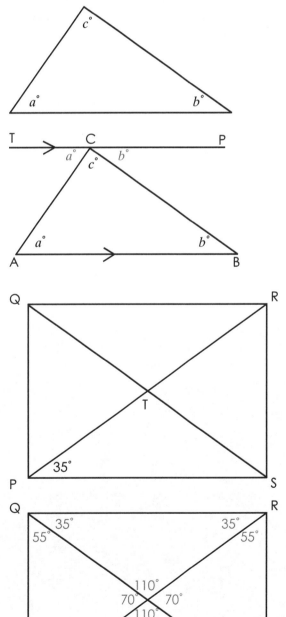

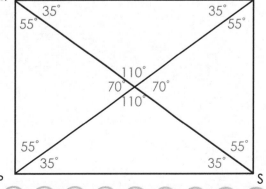

69

## BE ACTIVE

### QUICK TEST

1. A rhombus is a parallelogram whose diagonals intersect at right angles. Find all the angles in the diagram.

2. BC is parallel to DE. Calculate the size of ∠DAE

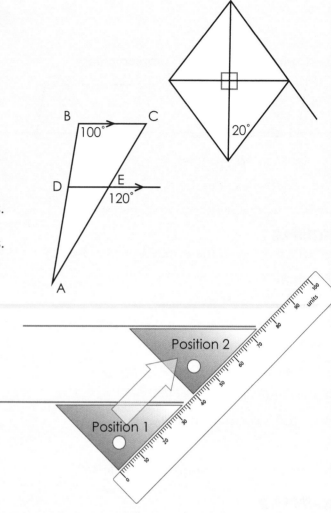

### QUICK TASKS

- It is important to be able to draw parallel lines. Before the advent of the computer drawing package, much use was made of set squares. One such set square was a plastic triangle whose angles were 45° and 90°.

  To draw a pair of parallel lines:

  Set the set square against a ruler (position 1)

  Draw a line as shown (red).

  Slide the set square along the ruler without letting the ruler turn to position 2. Draw another line.

  These two lines should be parallel. Explain.

  Explore how to draw a series of parallel lines which are 1 centimetre apart.

- Use the basic drawing tools to be found in Word to explore perspective drawing.

## OUR EVERYDAY LIVES:

To measure the height of a building you would want to measure ∠ABC. But how do you get your eye to B to make the measurement?

Long ago the surveyors placed a mirror at B, and when they saw the top of the building in the mirror they measured ∠FEB.

Prove that this is the same size as the angle we need.

(Hint: a ray will bounce off a mirror at the same angle that it hit it.)

**Response**

∠FEB = ∠EBH (alternate angles)

∠EBH = ∠ABC ( reflection)

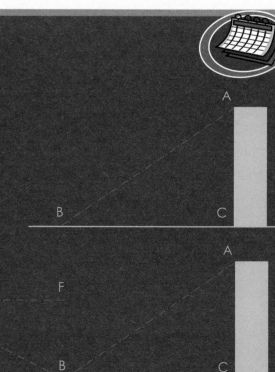

## DID YOU KNOW?

Eratosthenes was an ancient Greek famous for estimating the size of the Earth (as well as devising a method of finding prime numbers). He noticed that on midsummer day the Sun was directly overhead at noon (no shadows) in a town called Cyrene. 5000 stadia away (925 km) in Alexandria, the Sun was at an angle of 7° to the vertical, again measured using shadows.

How might this info be used to find the size of the Earth?

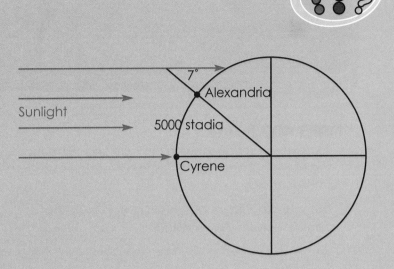

**Response**

The angle at the centre of the Earth is 7° (alternate angles).

If 7° gives a size of 5000 stadia on the surface then the full 360° will give a distance of 360 ÷ 7 × 5000 = 257 000 stadia (to the nearest 1000).

## MAKE THE LINK

71

- **Physics** – in the study of forces, we must be able to move the representative of the force to a new place in the drawing so that they can be added or subtracted.

- **Navigation** – in the study of bearings (see below) knowledge of related angles are essential, especially co-interior angles knowledge of which allows the easy calculation of back bearings.

- **Art** – the structure of a picture can be studied by considering perspective drawing. There is a line on the horizon called the eyeline. All the yellow lines are parallel to this. Lines which are at right angles to these in real life, look as if they are all converging on the one point on the horizon ... the vanishing point.

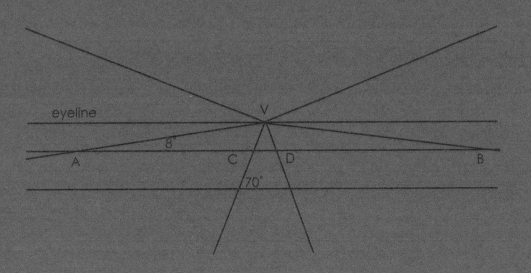

# PROPERTIES OF 2D SHAPES AND 3D OBJECTS

## MAPS AND PLANS

A previous section showed how, by changing the scale, we can represent very large triangles by smaller ones.

This scale should be quoted in any map so that it can be correctly interpreted.

### EXAMPLE 1

In this aerial photo 1 cm represents 100 m

(a) What is the actual distance between A and B?

(b) What distance on the photo would represent a real distance of 760 m?

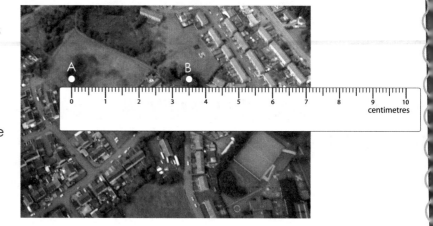

**Response**

(a) The distance AB measures as 3·5 cm

  1 cm represents 100 m

  so 3·5 cm represents 3·5 x 100 = 350 m

(b) 100 m is represented by 1 cm

  So 760 m is represented by 760 ÷ 100 = 7·6 cm.

72

In a map, **direction** is also important. Compass bearings are not accurate enough.

We make use of 3-figure bearings. The 3-figure bearing is the angle turned through clockwise, from North, to point in the direction you want to describe.

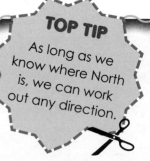

**TOP TIP**

As long as we know where North is, we can work out any direction.

**Examples**

The bearing of B from A is 130°

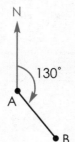

The bearing of Q from P is 240°

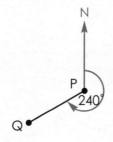

We often also need to know the return, or back bearing.

If the bearing of B from A is 065°, what is the bearing of A from B?

From our previous work we can see that 65° and $y°$ are co-interior angles and so supplementary. $y° = 180 - 65 = 115°$.

The return bearing $x = 360 - y = 360 - 115 = 245°$.

To make a map of a route, one should divide the route into 'legs' and describe the length and bearing of each. Of course nowadays, GPS is taking some of the difficulty out of the exercise.

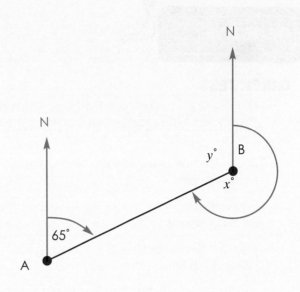

---

## EXAMPLE 2

I went on a sightseeing helicopter trip from Cumbernauld.

On the first leg of the trip we flew 25 km on a bearing of 220°.

We then went 20 km on a bearing of 120°. Our third leg was 10 km on a bearing of 050°.

For what distance and on what bearing should we fly to return directly to Cumbernauld?

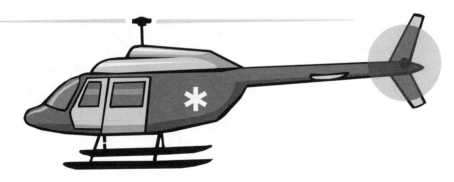

### Response
Pick a suitable scale, keeping in mind that the bigger the map is, the more accurate will be your answer. Let's say, 1 cm represents 5 km.

The table keeps the data tidy.

| Leg | Bearing | Distance | Scaled (÷ 5) cm |
|---|---|---|---|
| 1 | 220 | 25 | 5 |
| 2 | 120 | 20 | 4 |
| 3 | 50 | 10 | 2 |

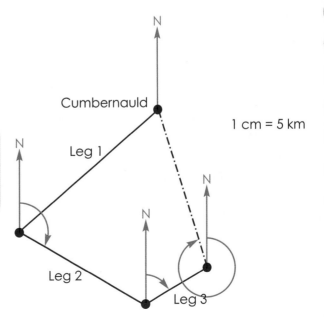

1 cm = 5 km

Measuring, we get a scaled distance of 4·9 cm for the leg home.

4·9 x 5 = 24·5 km and a bearing of 339°.

**BE ACTIVE**

## QUICK TEST

1. What distance is represented by 6·4 cm when the scale of the map is that 1 cm represents 10 km?

2. If 7·4 cm represents 185 km what is the scale of the map?

3. If the bearing from A to B is 74°, what is the bearing from B to A?

4. A yacht leaves port on a bearing of 055° sailing for 8 km.

   It then sailed for a further 9 km on a bearing of 240°.

   (a) Make a scale drawing of the journey.
   (b) How far from port is the yacht?

## QUICK TASKS

- The ancient Egyptians enlarged pictures by using grids.

  The small picture has a grid drawn on it.

  A larger grid with the same number of squares was drawn. A square at a time, the picture was copied into the larger grid.

  Get a picture and see if you can enlarge it by the same technique. You'll get an idea of the benefits of using a grid, and of the difficulties.

- The drawing tools of Word can be used to (a) copy a picture and (b) enlarge it by any factor you wish. See if you can find out how to do it.

- You can photograph your house with a digital camera and use the photos to make scale drawings of each face. You can then get the scale of each face the same. You can print out each face and then cut out and make a model of your house.

- A pantograph is a device to help you enlarge pictures. Look into this. See if you can obtain one. Can you work out why it works?

74

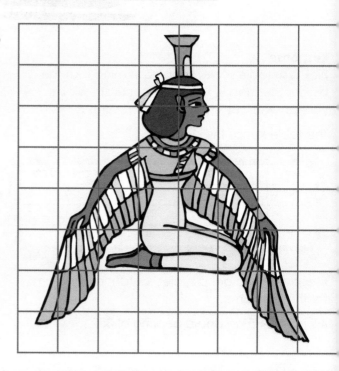

## MAKE THE LINK

- **Geography** – making maps and plans are an important facet of Geography. These maps are built around initial surveys not dissimilar from the dead reckoning techniques.

- **History** – maps and plans are often used when discussing battles and campaigns.

- **Craft and Design** – part of the design process is the need to make accurate scale drawings of the object being made.

- **Art** – the grid as a tool of enlargement is a technique used in art.

## DID YOU KNOW?

If you don't have access to GPS but you wish to keep track of where you are, you can make use of 'dead reckoning'. At regular times through the journey, you use a compass to find your bearings and you use your speed to find the distance travelled. A scale drawing is made, overlaid on a map, and continually updated to let you know where you are.

## OUR EVERYDAY LIVES:

- During times of conflict, fighting units are often asked to maintain radio silence. If the enemy could detect your signal it could give your position away.

  A special aerial would tell a listener the bearing of the radio. If there were two such listeners the position could be pinpointed.

  Two listeners, Agent X and Agent Y, were 8 km apart. Y was on a bearing of 070° from X. X detected the strongest signal on a bearing of 040°. Y picked it up on a bearing or 300°.

  Make a scale drawing to help you pinpoint the radio. How far is it from the line joining A to B?

  **Response**

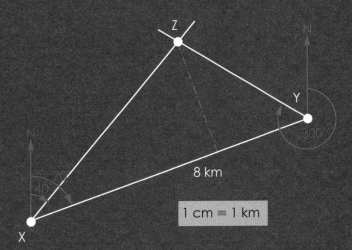

1 cm ≡ 1 km

A scale drawing, 1 cm represents 1 km, is drawn.

The radio's position is pinpointed and the distance, the dotted line, can be measured and scaled up, 3·1 km.

# ANGLES, SYMMETRY AND TRANSFORMATION

### CO-ORDINATES

In 1637 a Frenchman, René Descartes, described a method of describing position and shape which is used to this day in computer graphics packages and in computer animations such as the movie *Toy Story*. The French are so proud of their son that they named a street after him in Paris and issued a stamp depicting him and his book.

There is even a crater on the Moon named after him.

His idea was to realise that position can be described using coordinates.

Two directions are identified: the *x*-**direction** and the *y*-**direction**, which are at right angles to each other. A place to start is decided.

Thereafter every position can be described by saying how far in the *x*-direction and how far in the *y*-direction you have to go to get to it.

### EXAMPLE

To get to the point labelled A, we have to go 3 steps in the *x*-direction followed by 5 steps in the *y*-direction.

Rather than write this out every time, we write A(3, 5)... a lot shorter, but we have to agree that the first number is the steps in the *x*-direction and the second is the steps in the *y*-direction.

3 is called the *x*-**co-ordinate** of A.

5 is the *y*-**co-ordinate** of A.

The place to start is called the **origin** and has coordinates O(0, 0).

Two lines are drawn through the origin to indicate the *x*-direction and the *y*-direction.

These are called the *x*-axis and the *y*-axis respectively (the plural is 'axes').

The diagram is often called a co-ordinate diagram or, in honour of René Descartes, a Cartesian diagram.

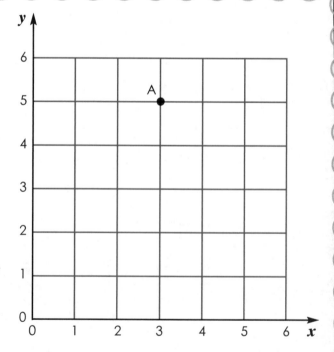

## EXAMPLE 1

(a) Draw the shape whose vertices have coordinates A(1, 2), B(9, 4), C(11, 10) and D(3, 8).

(b) What kind of shape is it?

(c) At which point do its diagonals intersect?

**Response**

(a)

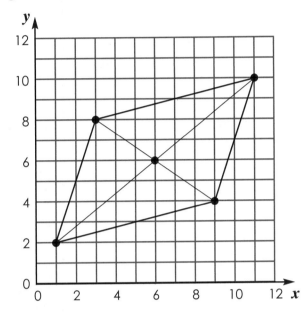

(b) a parallelogram

(c) (6, 6)

The coordinates of the points can be fractions.

## EXAMPLE 2

Plot the list of points below, joining them up as you go. Colour in the shape to make a silhouette of a well-known animal.

(1, 0), (2, 0), (1, 1), (3, 2), (8, 2), (8, 2·5), (7, 3), (8, 4), (9, 4·5), (9, 3), (10, 2), (11, 2), (10, 3), (9·5, 4), (9·5, 5), (10, 6), (11, 7), (11, 8), (10·5, 9), (11, 10), (11, 12), (10, 11), (9, 11), (8, 12), (8, 11), (8·5, 10), (8·5, 9), (4·5, 7·5), (3, 3), (1, 2), (0, 1), (1, 0).

**Response**

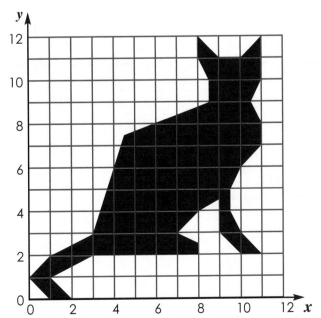

77

## BE ACTIVE

### QUICK TEST

1. (a) Name the features highlighted in the diagram.
   (b) What do we call (i) the red number
      (ii) the green number?
   (c) What direction is indicated by
      (i) the red arrow   (ii) the green arrow?

2. The points P(1, 2 ), Q(5, 9), R(9, 6) and S(9, 1) are the four vertices of a shape.
   (a Plot the points and draw the shape.
   (b) What kind of shape is it?
   (c) What are the coordinates of the point of intersection of its diagonals?

3. The diagram shows a V-kite.
   (a) State the coordinates of its vertices.
   (b) Which vertex has the smallest $x$-coordinate?
   (c) Which two vertices have the same $y$-coordinate?
   (d) Which two vertices would you join to draw its longer diagonal?

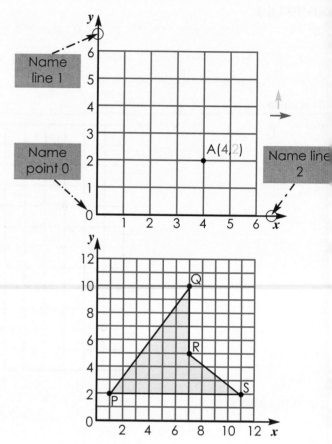

78

### QUICK TASK

1. You can get Excel spreadsheets to draw pictures.

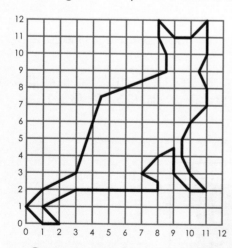

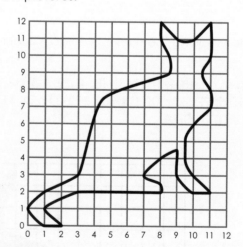

- Open a spreadsheet and in column A enter the x-coordinates of the shape you wish to draw and in column B put the corresponding y-coordinates. (In this example I've used the 'cat' from earlier.)
- Highlight the list (A2 to B33).
- Choose Insert > Chart ... and select XY (Scatter).
  If you now pick lines with no dots you'll get the first version.
  If you pick curves with no dots you'll get the smooth version.

| ⬩⬩ XY (Scatter) | ⧖ | ⧖ |

- Try to make some pictures of your own.

| ◇ | A | B |
|---|---|---|
| 1 | x | y |
| 2 | 1 | 0 |
| 3 | 2 | 0 |
| 4 | 1 | 1 |
| 5 | 3 | 2 |
| 6 | 8 | 2 |
| 7 | 8 | 2.5 |
| 8 | 7 | 3 |
| 9 | 8 | 4 |
| 10 | 9 | 4.5 |
| 11 | 9 | 3 |
| 12 | 10 | 2 |
| 13 | 11 | 2 |
| 14 | 10 | 3 |
| 15 | 9.5 | 4 |
| 16 | 9.5 | 5 |
| 17 | 10 | 6 |
| 18 | 11 | 7 |
| 19 | 11 | 8 |
| 20 | 10.5 | 9 |
| 21 | 11 | 10 |
| 22 | 11 | 12 |
| 23 | 10 | 11 |
| 24 | 9 | 11 |
| 25 | 8 | 12 |
| 26 | 8 | 11 |
| 27 | 8.5 | 10 |
| 28 | 8.5 | 9 |
| 29 | 4.5 | 7.5 |
| 30 | 3 | 3 |
| 31 | 1 | 2 |
| 32 | 0 | 1 |
| 33 | 1 | 0 |

## MAKE THE LINK

- **Physics** – As well as in the making of pictures, coordinates are used to explore connections between different things and to discover laws in science.

- **Geography** – Ordnance Survey co-ordinates – see Our Everyday Lives section for more details.

- **Computing** – Computer graphics make heavy use of coordinates; the screen is imagined as a grid of points called pixels.

- **Art** – The study of symmetry can be made easier by considering coordinates and how to change them to create effects.

## DID YOU KNOW?

In the previous section we saw how the Egyptians used grids to enlarge pictures. The same idea can be carried out using coordinates. If a shape can be defined by giving the coordinates of its vertices, then it can be doubled in size if we double its coordinates.

### Example
Make a version of the arrow, twice as big.

### Response
The vertices of the original arrow are:

(1, 0), (1, 4), (0, 4), (2, 6), (4, 4), (3, 4), (3, 0)

Double each coordinate.

(2, 0), (2, 8), (0, 8) (4, 12), (8, 8), (6, 8), (6, 0)

Now plot the new points.

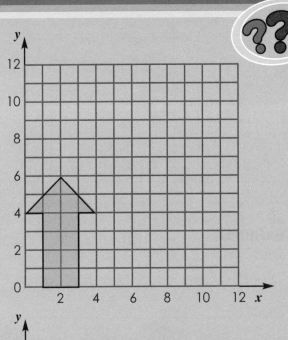

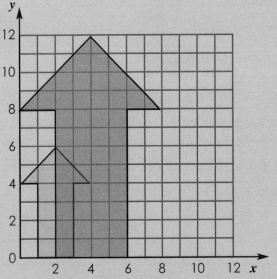

79

## OUR EVERYDAY LIVES:

Ordnance Survey grid references are simply coordinates in disguise. When a geographer thinks of the grid reference 4531, the mathematician thinks (45, 31) or if they use 6-figure references, e.g. 451316, the mathematician thinks (45·1, 31·6).

# ANGLES, SYMMETRY AND TRANSFORMATION

## SYMMETRY

Many computer drawing packages, including the simple one included with Microsoft Word, provide the facility to flip images horizontally and to flip vertically.

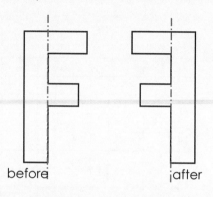

before          after

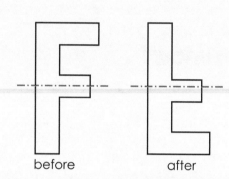

before          after

**80**

## EXAMPLES

You can certainly tell the 'before' and 'after' images apart.

Here is a flower, flipped horizontally and also flipped vertically.

original          flipped horizontally          flipped vertically

See that after the horizontal flip there is no change... it still looks the same. We say the flower has a vertical axis of symmetry... or line of symmetry.

We can sort shapes out by the lines of symmetry they have:

Examine this rectangle:

Flipped horizontally or vertically it looks the same, but flip it with the axis on a diagonal and it looks different.

A rectangle has only 2 axes of line symmetry:

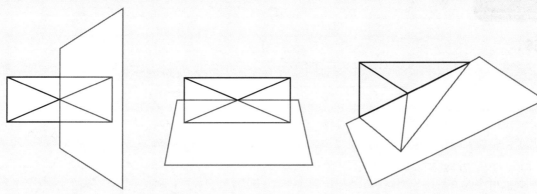

You can use the fact that a shape has symmetry to solve problems.

## EXAMPLE 1

The diagonals of a rhombus are both axes of symmetry of the rhombus. Calculate the sizes of the 4 angles of the rhombus.

**Response**

Using the horizontal axis of symmetry we get:

Then using the vertical axis we get:

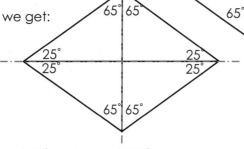

The rhombus has two angles of 50° and two of 130°.

## EXAMPLE 2

A kite has one axis of symmetry. Calculate its perimeter.

**Response**

By symmetry:

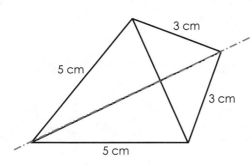

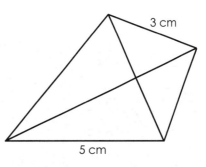

So the perimeter = 3 + 5 + 3 + 5 = 16 cm

81

**BE ACTIVE**

### QUICK TEST

1.  Make a sketch of a square and draw its axes of symmetry.

2.  Draw a trapezium
    (i)  with one axis of symmetry
    (ii)  with no axes of symmetry.

3.  How many axes of symmetry does a parallelogram have?

4.  The V-kite shown has one axis of symmetry.
    (a) Find all its angles.
    (b) Calculate its perimeter.

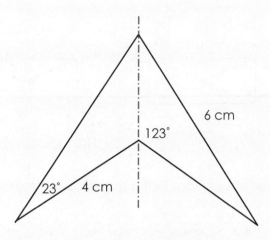

### QUICK TASK

*   Flowers are a good source of symmetry.

    Here is a flower which has five lines of symmetry.

    Make a poster of flowers which show 1, 2, 3, 4, 5 and 6-fold symmetry.

*   Explore how by paper folding and cutting, you can create symmetrical patterns. Fold it so that the finished pattern has 1 axis, 2 axes, 3 axes, 4 axes, five axes or 6 axes. (1,2 and 4 should be easy; 3 and 6 are related; 5 is difficult.)

82

### MAKE THE LINK

*   **Physics** – the study of Optics and Light requires a good understanding of reflection.

*   **Chemistry** – atomic structures can be categorised by referring to the symmetries of the crystal.

*   **Geology** – in the study of fossil shells, the geologist tells types of shells apart by using symmetry. Brachiopods have a line of symmetry across the back of the shell. Bivalves have a line of symmetry between the two parts (or valves) of the shell.

*   **Botany** – symmetry can help us tell families of plants apart.

*   **Art** – symmetry plays a big part in various branches of art. Salvador Dalí in his famous work 'Swans reflecting Elephants', made very good use of it to surprise the observer. Look it up on the internet.

## DID YOU KNOW?

Here is a puzzle invented by Henry Dudeney, a well known Victorian puzzler. A milkmaid milks the cow at A and takes the pail of milk to the dairy at B. She always makes a detour to the river. Why she does that is a mystery. Your task is to draw the shortest route between A and B which touches the river at some point.

River

• B

A•

**Response**

The shortest distance between two points is a straight line.

Imagine the riverbank is a mirror. The shortest distance between A and B as described will be the same distance as the straight line joining A to the reflection of B in the 'mirror'.

The diagram should explain:

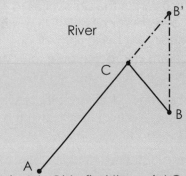

Join A to B' to find the point C. A to C to B is the shortest route. Note that by symmetry, CB' = CB.

The same 'trick' is used by snooker players when they have to bounce a ball off a cushion.

## OUR EVERYDAY LIVES:

For a very practical reason, many of the structures made by engineers are symmetrical.

When the shapes are symmetrical the forces and pressures tend to be balanced. This also allows the engineer to make many calculations.

**Example**

Motorway bridges often have line symmetry.

Once you have made measurements on one side of the motorway, you can deduce the corresponding measurements on the other side.

This diagram is a simplified view of a motorway bridge

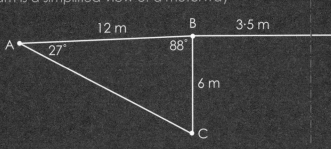

(a) What is the size of angle (i) ∠EFD (ii) ∠EDF?

(b) What is the length of the pillar ED?

(c) How long is the bridge from A to F?

# DATA AND ANALYSIS

## DATA COLLECTION

In 1854 Florence Nightingale went to Turkey to help improve hospital conditions for the wounded soldiers in the Crimean war.

She arrived to find the conditions appalling. She was only able to convince the authorities to give her funds to improve the hospitals in Crimea for the soldiers by keeping detailed records of casualties and deaths and being able to illustrate the information in a sensible way.

She was able to convince them that there were more people dying in the hospitals that in the battlefield.

The information she gathered couldn't be disputed... it was robust.

It was detailed and to the point (not vague).

It allowed her to make a clear link between the unsanitary conditions and the fatalities.

The information itself was a massive set of facts and figures, unstructured and difficult to interpret by the people she wanted to convince. She developed tables and charts which dramatically illustrated the details in a plain way for all to see.

When we work on a project we should try and remember Florence Nightingale's methods. The best way to learn about data handling is to do such a project and then make a presentation of your findings.

You should make up a question, the answer to which interests you.

Collect the data you think will help you answer the question.

Sort it and analyse it.

Look for conclusions.

Make charts that might help you illustrate the data or the conclusion.

---

### EXAMPLE

*The question:*

Should you be buying live recordings if you have bought all the studio recordings?

*Collecting the data:*

We can't examine all the live performances of a group so we take a sample. We will then make the assumption that the sample is typical of the group's performance and that any findings hold good for all their work. How big should the sample be?

If we only looked at one track no one would have confidence in our findings.

If we looked at 20 tracks there would be more confidence in the conclusions. We say the findings are more robust. The bigger the sample, the more accurate our findings, but the longer it will take to arrive at them. Since time is money, the bigger the sample, the more expensive the survey. We tend to compromise between robustness and cost. Sometimes the source of the data favours one conclusion rather than another. We should be guarded against such biased sources.

One would expect that the official site of the group would contain the most reliable raw data on this field, though you wouldn't use it to find out how popular the group is.

## EXAMPLE (CONTINUED)

### Collecting the data (cont.):

The play list of a live recording of a concert was examined.

The duration of each live track was compared with the duration of the equivalent studio recording.

Assuming the group performs equally as well in a concert as in the studio, we felt that a longer duration would be a positive thing.

The raw data was collected by searching the net for the band's official site, hopefully the source of the most reliable, dependable figures.

The times are given in minutes and seconds with the studio times in brackets.

1. 'Jumpin' Jack Flash' – 4:23(3:42)
2. 'Shattered' – 4:06(3:47)
3. 'She Was Hot' – 4:44(4:41)
4. 'All Down the Line' – 4:35(3:49)
5. 'Loving Cup' – 4:02(4:23)
6. 'As Tears Go By'– 3:32(2:43)
7. 'Some Girls' – 4:19(4.37)
8. 'Imagination' – 6:39(4:38)
9. 'Tumbling Dice' – 4:24(3:45)
10. 'You Got the Silver' – 3:22(2:50)

11. 'Sympathy for the Devil' – 5:56(6:24)
12. 'Start Me Up' – 4:05(3:32)
13. 'Brown Sugar' – 5:25(3:49)
14. '(I Can't Get No) Satisfaction' – 5:37(3:43)
15. 'Paint It Black' – 4:28(3:46)
16. 'Undercover of the Night' – 4:24 (4:32)
17. 'Little T&A' – 4:09(3:23)
18. 'I'm Free' – 3:31(2:23)
19. 'Shine a Light' – 4:05(4:14)
20. 'The Last Time' – 3:08(3:42)
21. 'Little Red Rooster' – 5.15(3:05)
22. 'Time Is on My Side' – 3:39(2:59)

85

## DATA AND ANALYSIS

### EXAMPLE (CONTINUED)

*Analysing the data:*

The findings should be organised in a table. Here are the first 4 tracks done:

| Track | Live (m s) | minutes | studio (m s) | minutes | difference |
|---|---|---|---|---|---|
| 1 | 4 23 | 4·3833 | 3 42 | 3·7 | 0·6833 |
| 2 | 4 06 | 4·1 | 3 47 | 3·78333 | 0·3167 |
| 3 | 4 44 | 4·7333 | 4 41 | 4·6833 | 0·05 |
| 4 | 4 35 | 4·5833 | 3 49 | 3·8167 | 0·7667 |

A spreadsheet is being used to help with the arithmetic.

Minutes and seconds are being converted to minutes only.

B2 holds the duration of the first track with minutes and seconds separated by a space. (4 23). Two digits are used to record seconds.

C2 has a formula to do the conversion: $= LEFT(B2,1)+RIGHT(B2,2)/60$

Similar entries and formulae are made for the studio times.

F2 holds a formula to work out the difference between live and studio times: $=C2-E2$

At the other end of the table, we have …

| 21 | 5 15 | 5 ·25 | 3 05 | 3·0833 | 2·1667 |
|---|---|---|---|---|---|
| 22 | 3 39 | 3·65 | 2 59 | 2·9833 | 0·6667 |
| sum | | 97·8 | | 84·45 | 13·35 |
| average | | 4·45 | | 3·84 | 0·61 |

The second last row works out some totals using the formula $=SUM(C2:C23)$ in C24 and similar in E24 and F24.

The last row works out some means (averages) using the formula $= AVERAGE(C2:C23)$ in C25 and similar in E25 and F25.

In this form the data set is easier to interpret.

*Drawing conclusions:*

On average a live track is 0·61 minutes longer that the same studio track.

All 22 tracks end up a total of 13·35 minutes longer… that is 13·35 minutes out of a 97·8-minute concert.

$13·35 \div 97·8 \times 100 \approx 14\%$ extra.

The group does seem to offer better value for money in their live recordings.

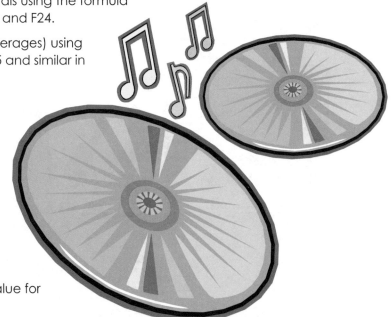

## EXAMPLE (CONTINUED)

*Illustrating the data:*

**For a presentation, a chart should be made of the relevant data.**

You can use the Chart Wizard of the spreadsheet to do this. It can then be cut and pasted into your presentation.

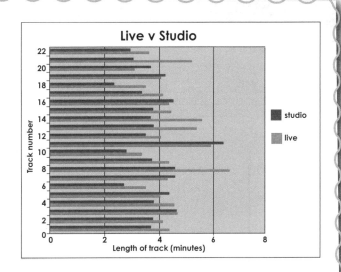

**Be careful to avoid misleading charts.**

The chart opposite would seem to suggest that live recordings were twice as long as studio recordings. The reader has to really look at the *y*-axis to see that it doesn't start at zero but at 75 minutes.

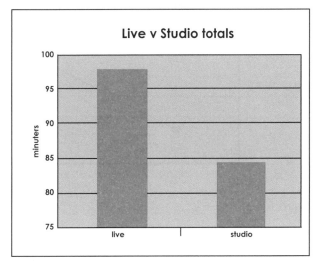

87

If you start a project trying to prove that live tracks are longer you are liable to let your prejudice accept this as a valid chart.

The charts below would be better... the right-hand one takes advantage of the formatting facilities of the spreadsheet.

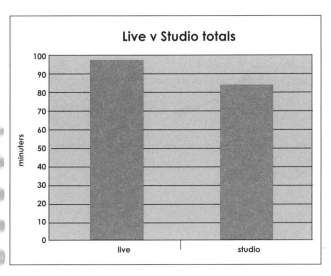

**BE ACTIVE**

## QUICK TEST

1.  Calculate the mean of each data set correct to one decimal place.
    (i) 1, 2, 4, 6, 8
    (ii) 3·4 seconds, 2·6 seconds, 4·3 seconds, 5·5 seconds, 2·2 seconds, 3·0 seconds.
2.  Look at each of the charts and suggest a reason why they might be considered misleading.
    (i)

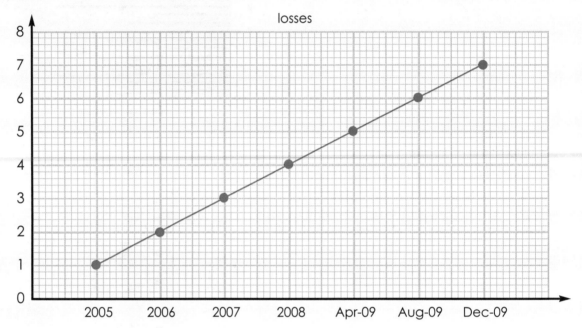

    (ii)

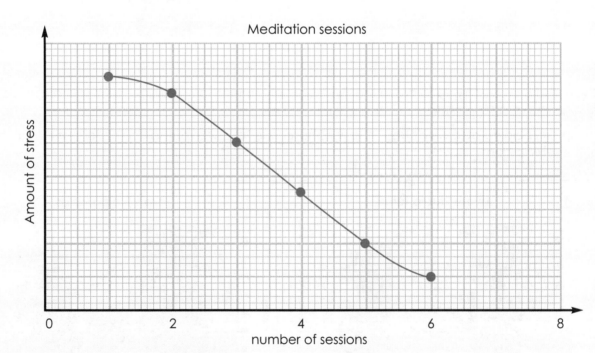

3.  Why might the following lead to biased samples?
    (i) You phone round to ask how the 'Credit Crunch' is affecting people.
    (ii) You hop on buses to conduct a survey on traffic.
    (iii) You stand outside the cinema and ask about the public's viewing habits.

88

**BE ACTIVE**

## QUICK TASKS

- Decide what interests you – football, rugby, music – and conduct a survey. Collect the data and organise it. Analyse it and draw conclusions.

- Set up a 'weather station' collecting data on rainfall, sunshine and wind strength for a month. Write a report at the end of the month illustrating the data you collected with the aid of charts.

- Explore the potential of Excel to make tables and charts.

## MAKE THE LINK

- **Physics** – scientific experiments are often a controlled way of collecting data. Analysing the data leads to the discovery of 'laws' that can be used for prediction.

- **Geography** – various facets of Geography depend on statistics and data handling.

- **Meteorology** – the weather forecasts are all based on statistics collected over years.

- **Modern Studies** – opinion polls and their analysis and conclusions can be discussed.

- **Business Studies** – statistics are used here to try and make sense of changing markets.

- **Statistics** – you will see in the next section that the probability of an event happening can be estimated using a survey.

## DID YOU KNOW?

Watch out for opinion polls at election times. They often give the 'error' along with their predictions.

## OUR EVERYDAY LIVES:

This topic is all practical. The type of problem will affect the type of survey.

If the traffic engineers wish to explore the need for traffic-calming in an area they will do surveys on (i) the number of accidents in that area; (ii) the average speed of traffic passing through the area; (iii) the traffic density at different times.

The difference between what is actually happening and what your survey tells you is happening is called the sampling error. The bigger the sample, the smaller the error.

## IDEAS OF CHANCE AND UNCERTAINTY

### PROBABILITY

We all have an idea of the likelihood of an event.

We know that when we throw a standard die, it is **impossible** that it comes up 7. We know that when we drop a plate it is **certain** to fall down.

Some would say that when we drop a piece of toast it is certain to fall butter-side down... but that's another story.

We can say when something is likely and when it's unlikely. In many cases we can tell which of two outcomes is more likely.

These terms, though useful, are quite vague. What we need is a more precise measurement of likelihood.

When we perform an experiment like tossing a coin or casting a die each outcome is equally likely. Under these circumstances we define the probability of an event, E, as:

$$P(E) = \frac{\text{number of ways E can occur}}{\text{total number of things that can occur}}$$

### EXAMPLE

Here are 14 playing cards (see photo). What is the probability that if one is selected at random

(i)   it is a 3?

(ii)  it is higher than a 5?

(iii) it is red?

(iv) it is not a spade?

### Response

(i)   $P(3) = \frac{\text{number of 3s}}{\text{number of cards}} = \frac{2}{14} = \frac{1}{7} = 0{\cdot}14$ to 2 d.p.

(ii)  $P(\text{card} > 5) = \frac{\text{number of cards} >5}{\text{number of cards}} = \frac{8}{14} = \frac{4}{7} = 0{\cdot}57$ to 2 d.p.

(iii) $P(\text{card is red}) = \frac{\text{number of red cards}}{\text{number of cards}} = \frac{6}{14} = \frac{3}{7} = 0{\cdot}43$ to 2 d.p.

(iv) $P(\text{card not spade}) = \frac{\text{number of cards not spades}}{\text{number of cards}} = \frac{9}{14} = 0{\cdot}64$ to 2 d.p.

An event will either happen or it won't. This is a **certainty**. So the probability that something will happen plus the probability that it won't is equal to 1.

If we know the probability of something happening then, by subtracting this from 1, we can work out the probability that it won't happen.

Sometimes, though you can't count the ways, you can still find the probability. For example a teacher has two different lengths of dried spaghetti. He picks one up at random and snaps it in two to give him three pieces. What is the probability that he can use the three pieces to form a triangle?

### Response

You can't count the number of ways the teacher can make the break. However, with a bit of thought we realise that if you break the bigger bit you can always make a triangle. If you break the smaller bit you can never make a triangle.

If the teacher chooses at random then:

$P(\text{making a triangle}) = P(\text{picking the longer piece}) = \frac{\text{number of longer pieces}}{\text{number of pieces}} = \frac{1}{2}$

**BE ACTIVE**

## QUICK TESTS

1. Calculate the probability that when a ten-faced dice is cast, the number will be divisible by 3.

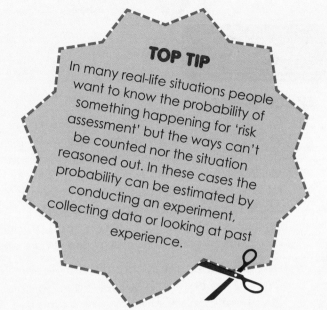

**TOP TIP**

In many real-life situations people want to know the probability of something happening for 'risk assessment' but the ways can't be counted nor the situation reasoned out. In these cases the probability can be estimated by conducting an experiment, collecting data or looking at past experience.

2. Traffic lights are set to go through a fixed cycle with each setting lasting a fixed time:

| 60 seconds | 5 seconds | 60 seconds | 5 seconds |

What is the probability that
(i) you'll arrive at the lights when they are green?
(ii) you'll see a red light?

3. An ice-cream vendor sells four flavours. The table records his last 50 sales.

| Flavour | Number sold |
|---|---|
| vanilla | 17 |
| lime | 18 |
| chocolate | 6 |
| cider | 9 |
| Total | 50 |

What is the probability that the next customer
(i) wants a chocolate ice cream?
(ii) doesn't want vanilla or lime?

91

**BE ACTIVE**

## QUICK TASKS

* Conduct a survey on traffic movement near your school. Work out the probability of a car going by in any minute. Observe for 10 minutes. Make a table up with two columns; column 1 for which minute and column 2 for the car count in that minute. You can then get estimates for the probability of no cars passing in a minute, 1 car passing in a minute, 2 cars, etc.

  Do these probabilities change at different times of the day? Alternatively you can do this at traffic lights, examining how long the queue gets when the lights are at red.

* Examine the sets of letters in the game of Scrabble.

  Work out the probability of picking out each letter and compare it with the score you get for using that letter. Comment on any connection you see.

  Get a book and pick a page at random.

  Make a count of how often each letter turns up. Work out the probability that a letter chosen at random will be an A, B, C, etc. How closely do these probabilities match those in Scrabble?

  The information found here can be used to crack some secret codes. Look up Caesar Shift on the internet.

* You can use Excel to help you with experiments by simulating tossing coins or casting dice.

  **Simulating a die:**
  In A1 type: =ROUND(RAND()*5+1,0)

  Fill right to column E and down to row 20.

  You should now have a hundred 'throws of the dice'.

  Make a table like this with the word 'score' in A22:

| Score | Frequency | Probability |
|-------|-----------|-------------|
| 1 | | |
| 2 | | |
| 3 | | |
| 4 | | |
| 5 | | |
| 6 | | |
| total | | |

In B23 type: =COUNTIF($A$1:$E$20,A23)

Fill down to B28

In B29 type: =SUM(B23:B28)

In C23 type: =B23/$B$29

Fill down to C28

The table will do all the counting for you and work out the experimental probabilities for you to compare with the theoretical value.

**Simulating a coin:**
In A1 type: =ROUND(RAND()*1+1,0)

Fill right to column E and down to row 20.

You should now have a hundred results, a mix of 1s and 2s.

Let 1 stand for Heads and 2 for Tails.

Make a table like this with the word 'score' in A22:

| Score | Frequency | Probability |
|-------|-----------|-------------|
| 1 | | |
| 2 | | |
| total | | |

In B23 type: =COUNTIF($A$1:$E$20,A23)

Fill down to B24

In B29 type: =SUM(B23:B24)

In C23 type: =B23/$B$25

Fill down to C24

**Try and simulate other events**
Suppose a fire alarm is conducted at random on 1 day of the week.

Suppose we are interested in the chances of it happening on a Friday.

In A1 type: =ROUND(RAND()*4+1,0)

Let 1,2,3,4 stand for NOT Friday and 5 stand for Friday.

See if you can figure out how to end up with a table like this:

| Score | Frequency | Probability |
|-------|-----------|-------------|
| Not Friday | | |
| Friday | | |
| total | | |

## MAKE THE LINK

- **Physics** – some experiments can be too difficult to tackle in school and may well be simulated. To perform the simulation the probability of each outcome should be known.

- **Geography** – again simulation is used to create many of the computer models of economic systems ... games such as SIMCITY use simulation.

- **Meteorology** – the weather forecasts are based on past statistics and the likelihood of their being correct is calculated by running simulations over and over hundreds of times.

- **Business Studies** – risk assessment depends on probabilities being known.

- **Statistics** – the Theory of Probability will be developed partially based on these beginnings.

- **Computing** – the activity above shows a little of how probabilities can be calculated and simulations developed.

## DID YOU KNOW?

In America Groundhog Day (2nd February) was made famous by the movie of the same name. If the groundhog comes out of its hole and can see its shadow there is going to be another 6 weeks of winter weather. If it doesn't see its shadow then there is going to be good weather and an early spring.

One study looked at weather records kept for 40 years and found that in 15 of those years the weather pattern fitted the description. What is the probability that the groundhog will be right?

**Response**
We treat the fraction of the time the groundhog was right as the probability.

$$P(\text{Groundhog correct}) = \frac{\text{number of times correct}}{\text{number of times examined}} = \frac{15}{40} = (0.38 \text{ to 2 d.p.})$$

## OUR EVERYDAY LIVES:

In real life, probability is used to guide those who have to make risk assessments.

As well as probability of an event happening, these people have to consider the consequences of the event happening.

**Example**
Suppose the consequence of a piece of machinery breaking down is that a replacement will have to be bought, costing £50.

Suppose that the probability of it breaking down in any given year is 0·1. This means it will break down once in 10 years. You can spread the cost over the 10 years, 50 ÷ 10 = £5 a year.

Some would say that's not a lot and it's probably not worth spending money on research and improvement to make the probability of breakdown smaller.

Suppose, however, that the breakdown causes the factory to stop working for a week or two with losses running to £1 000 000. This works out at £100 000 a year. It would definitely be worthwhile paying for research to decrease the probability of failure.

# ANSWERS * ANSWERS * ANSWERS * ANSWERS *

**Page 7**
1. (a) 350 (b) 590 (c) 800 (d) 3460
2. (a) 5·67 (b) 0·22 (c) 0·02 (d) 9·01
3. (a) 7300 (b) 4·9 **note: not 4·90** (c) 0·028
   (d) 0·0014

**Page 11**
1. 3·91 + 4·20 = 8·11; 12·26 − 8·11 = 4·15
2. 106·25 ÷ 17 = 6·25; 6·25 × 24 = 150
3. 34·89 + 41·27 = 76·16; 100 − 76·16 = 23·84;
   23·84 ÷ 2 = 11·92

**Page 13**
1. 49·05
2. 27·85
3. 1, 8, 27, 64, 125, 216, 343, 512, 729, 1000
4. 12·54

**Page 15**
1. (a) −3 (b) −5 (c) −3 (d) 2
2. (a) 7 (b) −9 (c) −2 (d) 4
3. (a) −10 (b) 18 (c) −14 (d) 81
4. (a) −5 (b) 3 (c) −4 (d) 3·5

**Page 17**
1. (a) 7 (b) 1 (c) 16 (d) 126
2. (a) 75 (b) 105 (c) 126 (d) 396
3. 26 ml
4. Yes. After 240 minutes.

**Page 19**
1. (a) yes (b) yes (c) yes (d) no
2. (a) 64 (b) 64 (c) 25 (d) 216
3. 30

**Page 21**
1. (a) $\frac{2}{5}$ (b) 0·4 or 0·40 (c) 40%
2. 39

**Page 23**
1. (a) $\frac{6}{35}$ (b) $\frac{15}{18} = \frac{5}{6}$
2. (a) $8\frac{1}{4}$ (b) $1\frac{1}{2}$

**Page 25**
1. $\frac{15}{28}$
2. $\frac{7}{20}$
3. (a) $4\frac{24}{30}$ (b) $2\frac{13}{30}$
4. (a) United: $\frac{11}{14}$ = 0·7857 ... Rovers: $\frac{16}{21}$ = 0·7619
   United better

   (b) United: $\frac{11}{22}$ = 0·5 ... Rovers: $\frac{7}{15}$ = 0·4666
   United better

(c) United: $\frac{22}{36}$ = 0·6111 ... Rovers: $\frac{23}{36}$ = 0·63888
Rovers better???
We are not adding fractions.

**Page 27**
1. £12·80, £32·00
2. 9:1, 4:1, 7:3, 3:2, 1:1, 2:3, 3:7, 1:4, 1:9
3. 2:3

**Page 29**
1. Loam 35 litres; peat 15 litres; sand 10 litres
2. Loam 20 potfuls; peat 25 potfuls; sand 10 potfuls.

**Page 31**
1. £760·41 − £650 = £110·41
2. £5435·77 − £4500 = £935·77
3. 16·1%
4. Convert each to an APR
   (i) 16·8% (ii) 17% (iii) 15·2%.
   So (iii) is best deal.

**Page 33**
1. 823·0 m/min (49·4 km/h)

**Page 35**
1. 938 692 500 km
2. 39·27 seconds

**Page 37**
1. (a) 16.6 m (b) 35 min
2. 41·6 million kilometres
3. (a) 0·01 cm or 0·1 mm (b) 0·0002 cm or
   0·002 mm out
4. 1·4 km
5. (a) 9·8 cm (b) 10·8 cm

**Page 39**
1. (a) 7·85 cm (b) 9·14 cm

**Page 41**
1. (a) 4·32 cm$^2$ (b) 20 cm$^2$

**Page 43**
1. (a) 12·96 m$^2$ (b) 12·96 mm$^2$ (c) 49·5 km$^2$
   (d) 34·51 cm$^2$ (e) 78·54 m$^2$ (to 2 d.p.)

**Page 45**
1. 25·13 + 6·28 + 80·5 = 112 cm$^2$ to nearest cm$^2$.

**Page 47**
1. (a) 27 cm$^3$ (b) 30 cm$^3$ (c) 157·1 cm$^3$ (d) 30 cm$^3$

**Page 49**
1. (a) 27 cm$^3$ (b) 30 cm$^3$ (c) 157·1 cm$^3$
2. 170 m$^3$

**Page 51**

1. (a) 7, 11, 15, 19, 23
   (b) 2, 7, 12, 17, 22
   (c) 74, 71, 68, 65, 62
   (d) 2, 5, 10, 17, 26
   (e) 1, 2, 3, 16, 53
2. (a) the triangular numbers … the set with double-$n$ has the $(n + 1)$th triangular number in its set.
   (b) $t_7 = 28$
   (c) $t_{10} = 55$

**Page 53**

1. (a) $u_n = 2n + 4$
   (b) $u_n = 10n - 5$
   (c) $u_n = 23 - 3n$
   (d) $u_n = n^2 + 2$

**Page 56**

1. (a) $5a$
   (b) $5a + 3b$
   (c) $5x + 7$
   (d) $15x^2$
   (e) $24x2y$
   (f) $\frac{5y}{2x}$
   (g) $4x + 12$

**Page 59**

1. (a) $x = 4$ (b) $c = 3$ c) $x = 8$ (d) $x = 40$ (e) $x = 6$
2. (a) $8x + 2·60$ (b) $8x + 2·60 = 5; x = 0·30$

**Page 61**

1. (a) 33 (b) 40 (c) 9
2. (a) $w + 2 \times 10^2 \times 12^3 = 345\ 600$ watts
   (b) $w = 2 \times 8^2 \times 8^3 = 65\ 536$ watts
   So total = 655 360 watts

**Page 67**

1. 5·1 cm
2. $\angle PQR = 77°$, $\angle QRP = 58°$
3. Perimeter = 21·7 cm
4. $\angle ABC = 81°$ or $19°$

**Page 70**

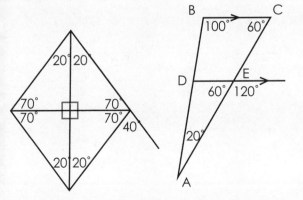

**Page 74**

1. 64 km
2. 1 cm represents 25 km
3. 254°
4. (a) student's own drawing (b) 1·2 km

**Page 78**

1. (a) line 1 is the $y$-axis, line 2 is the $x$-axis, point O is the origin.
   (b) (i) $x$-coordinate (ii) $y$-coordinate
   (c) (i) $x$-direction (ii) $y$-direction
2. (a)

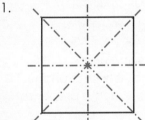

   (b) A kite (c) (7, 5)
3. (a) P(1, 2), Q(7, 10), R(7, 5), S(11, 2)
   (b) P (c) Q, R (d) Q, S

**Page 82**

1.

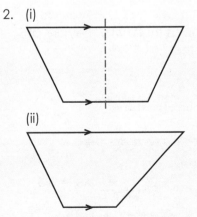

2. (i)

   (ii)

3. A parallelogram has no axes of symmetry.
4. (a) Completing the symmetry and using the fact that the angles of a triangle add up to 180°, we can complete the diagram. The four angles of the V-kite are: 23°, 23°, 68° and 246°.

95

(b) The perimeter = 4 + 6 + 6 + 4 = 20 cm

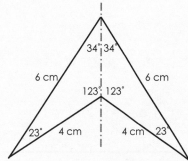

**Page 88**

1. (i) 4·2 (ii) 3·5 seconds

2. (i) The x-axis is being 'stretched' for 2009 hiding a leap in the losses. It should look like this:

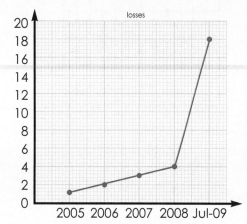

   (ii) the y-axis has no real meaning. The detail is too vague. What is being measured? What are the units?

3. (i) You only contact people with a phone.
   (ii) Sample is less likely to catch a proper set of car owners.
   (iii) You are most likely to get bias towards the genre of movie that is showing at that moment, as that's why they are at the cinema then.

**Page 91**

1. $P(3, 6, 9) = \frac{\text{number of multiples of 3}}{\text{number of possibilities}} = \frac{3}{10}$

2. (i) $P(\text{green}) = \frac{\text{green time}}{\text{time of cycle}} = \frac{60}{130} = \frac{6}{13}$
   $= 0·46$ to 2 d.p.
   (ii) $P(\text{any red}) = \frac{\text{red time}}{\text{time of cycle}} = \frac{65}{130} = \frac{1}{2} = 0·5$

3. (i) $P(\text{chocolate}) = \frac{\text{number of chocolate sales}}{\text{number of sales}} = \frac{6}{50} = 0·12$
   (ii) $P(\text{not vanilla or lime}) = \frac{\text{number of choc/cider sales}}{\text{number of sales}} = \frac{15}{30} = \frac{3}{10} = 0·3$